Everyone involved in the publication of this text has used his or her best efforts in preparing it. These efforts include the development, research, and testing of the theories and programs to determine their effectiveness. The author and publisher make no warranty of any kind, expressed or implied, with regard to these programs or the documentation contained in this book. The author and publisher shall not be liable in any event for incidental or consequential damages in connection with, or arising out of, the furnishing, performance, or use of these programs.

Trademark info:

Adobe® is a registered trademark of Adobe Systems Inc.

Windows® is a registered trademark of Microsoft.

Read In® is a registered trademark of Microsoft.

Microsoft Reader® is a registered trademark of Microsoft.

Adobe Acrobat® and Acrobat Reader® are registered trademarks of Adobe Systems Inc.

Poser® is a registered trademark of e Frontier America, Inc.

ISBN eBook 0-9778938-3-9

ISBN Paperback 0-9778938-4-7

Copyright © 2004, 2006 Timothy Sean Sykes

Forager Publications
2043 Cherry Laurel
Spring, TX 77386
www.foragerpub.com

AUTHOR'S NOTES

Where to Find the Required Files for Using This Text:

All of the files required to complete the lessons in this text can be downloaded free of charge from this site:

http://www.foragerpub.com/eBookFiles/

Links:

I designed this book as an eBook. Because of the utility of that format, eBook readers will find roughly 150+ inter- and extra-document links to make my readers' experiences more enjoyable. Obviously, I couldn't do the same in a printed text.

I have, however, exchanged most of the links with end-notes in the printed text, which I've numbered within the body of the text. You can use these to access the websites referenced in the eBook.

If you'd like to make it easy on yourself, open this file:

http://www.foragerpub.com/eBookFiles/Links.pdf

Here you'll find the same end notes, but these remain links to the associated references. Picking on them will save you a lot of typing!

Contacting the Author/Publisher:

Although we tried awfully hard to avoid errors, typos, and the occasional boo boos, I admit to complete fallibility. Should you find it necessary to let me know of my blunders, or to ask just about anything about the text – or even to make suggestions as to how to better the next edition, please feel free to contact me at: comments@foragerpub.com. I can't promise a fast response (although I'm usually pretty good about answering my email), but I can promise to read (almost) everything that comes my way.

In grateful memory of the fathers of self-reliance:

Henry David Thoreau
Ralph Waldo Emerson

And one of the first great self-publishers in the United States of America

Benjamin Franklin

Table of Contents

Lesson 1: Gaining a Basic Understanding of eBooks & PODs
What Is An eBook? 5
What Is A POD? 6
Why Use an eBook? 6
What Can I Expect Once I Create My eBook? 9
Summary 10

Lesson 2: Selecting a Format 11
I've Heard There Are Many Formats, which Should I Use? 12
What Will My Readers Experience With These Applications? 17
What About Security – I Don't Want People to Steal My Work? 55
Summary 57

Lesson 3: Gathering Your Tools 58
What Will I Need To Produce My eBook or POD? 59
What Will I Need To Market My eBook? 71
Publishers, Distributors, and Booksellers – A Brief Introduction 80
Summary 89

Lesson 4: Preparing Your Text 91
Preparing the Text 92
Laying Out Your Manuscript for Publication (Preparing the Appearance of Your eBook or POD) 95
Summary 107

Lesson 5: Converting Your Text 109
Converting to a Microsoft Reader Format 110
Converting to an Adobe or Acrobat Reader Format 117
Converting to a PDF Using the Adobe PDF Online Tool (Adobe eBooks or Print Files for PODs) 118
Converting to a PDF Using Adobe Acrobat Professional (or Standard), Release 6 or 7 127
A Word about Post-Conversion Editing 152
Summary 153

Lesson 6: What to Do with Your eBook or POD 154
Marketing and Distribution: What to Expect from the Pros 155
Outlets 156

    Pricing 165
    Know Your Representatives and Your Rights 168
    The Payoff – Getting Paid! 170
    Advertising 171
  Other Options – CDs and Audio Books 175
  Summary 177
Conclusion 179

Well, com'n in … check it out!

Every project has a beginning. Yours began when you made the decision to blow off the mega-publishing houses and do it yourself. This means two things – first, you believe in your work, and second, that you are determined to make it available for someone to read. I commend you for both.

It has been my experience over the years that a writer is often his or her own worst critic. (Only occasionally do I run into one who is right ... or worse, believes something is better than it actually is.) Unfortunately, it often takes the sales of hundreds or even thousands of books to get past the eternal feeling that your book might have been better if only you'd phrased this or that a little differently.

Xerox rejections from the major publishing houses don't help. The mega-publishers are swamped with books – often very good books (and occasionally stinkers) – by folks like us. But we don't have the connections or where-with-all to convince them to actually read our books, much less publish them. After all, even if they could read a book a day (hundreds of pages), that would limit them to 365 books a year (working Christmas and holidays). As much as I enjoy reading, that's beyond the scope of my abilities. It's probably beyond theirs as well. Then they're limited as to how much money they can spend publishing and marketing books; remember, the return on a book may not happen for a year or two (and occasionally never). Unless you're Stephen King, you're asking them to invest in less than a sure thing.

But despite all of this, you believe in your work – your textbooks and your stories and your professional papers. What's more, you're determined to make it available for students, colleagues, and readers of all ages and from all walks of life. And if the good Lord is willing, you'll make a dollar or two in the process!

That's why I'm here. I have created and sold hundreds of eBooks and PODs, and I'm going to help you do it, too. I'll remind you up front, however, that nothing is certain but taxes and hard work ... and expenses (after all, nothing is free!). But I'll show you where I cut corners and shaved expenses. Hopefully, you'll be able to do the same (and share any new tricks you discover along the way with me!).

It may hearten you to know that, as far as eBooks go, I was in the black (well, dark gray) within weeks of my first publication!

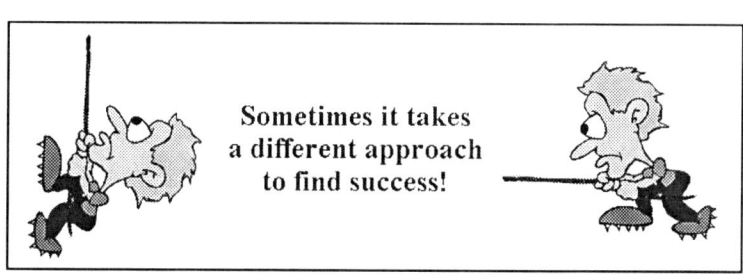

Lesson  1

Following this lesson, you will:

- ✓ *Know what an eBook is*
- ✓ *Know what a POD is*
- ✓ *Understand why you should create eBooks*
- ✓ *Know something about your target audience – who is going to read your eBook? Your POD?*

Gaining a Basic Understanding of eBooks & PODs

Let's start our training with the basics – what exactly are eBooks, what are PODs, of what use can they be to us, and can we justify the effort they'll take in terms of time and money.

Step 1.1   What Is An eBook?

An eBook (electronic book) is a paperless document or publication readable on any of a number of electronic instruments, such as computers or "handheld" devices. (Handheld devices include Pocket PCs, PDAs, Palm Pilots, eBook readers, and so forth – the market has even grown to include some cell phones.) Depending on your budget and understanding, you may be reading the eBook version of this text right now!

Dell Axim X5 Image Courtesy of Dell. Inc

The most popular handheld devices include the Dell Axim (shown above), which sells for about $400, and the HP iPAQ, which at this printing, still starts at about $300. Other companies sell handheld devices, too, and the price range pretty much covers the spectrum. But I'd stick with one of the name brands that utilize a Windows operating system. Since they're the most popular, that's where your market lies.

If you've written a work of fiction or a text which contains few graphics, I suggest picking up a handheld device. You can generally find an inexpensive, black and white device for around $100 if you look for it. (Try shopping eBay for a deal.) It helps if you can find the time to read a book or two on it as well – if not for the enjoyment of the book then for the experience. Remember, many readers will use a device like this to read your book. (Also remember, it's tax deductible!)

Step 1.2 What Is A POD?

POD publishers have developed technology that allows us to print books while minimizing the cost of inventory control, printing costs, and even the cost in harvested trees. This technology – Print on Demand (POD) – simply means that we don't have to print a book until someone wants it. Because of the speed of this new technology, the buyer hardly notices that the book didn't exist when he ordered it!

Several companies – POD Houses – exist that can help you take advantage of this technology ... for a price. We'll discuss them alongside the eBook business over the course of this text.

The two are fairly closely related. That is, they both serve the self-publisher as well as the mega-publisher; they both open the publishing world to those of us who don't have zillions of dollars to invest but do have work worthy of publication; and *preparation for one closely parallels preparation for the other.*

Step 1.3 Why Use an eBook?

As with any new technology, eBooks have their pluses and minuses.

Trees have better uses!

Chief among the pluses lies the issue of environmental awareness – when I "asked Jeeves"[1] how many trees it took to create a book, I discovered that one average tree produced between 123 and

256 books (of about 750 pages each). Of course, that doesn't include all the other considerations (power to run the presses and such). An electronic book doesn't require all that – just a few rechargeable batteries to run the reader. (Of course, that's another environmental issue, but we won't go there.)

Then there's the profit margin to consider. The cost of a book drops tremendously when you eliminate the need to cut down trees, turn them into pulp and paper, and so forth. The 1200 page, printed version of my AutoCAD textbook sold for some $63 (of which I got about $3). The first eBook version increased to some 1400 pages (formatting concerns which we'll talk about later) and required a Part I and Part II (file size concerns – again, we'll talk about all that later). Each sold for $9.95 ($19.90 for the entire book). I made about $4.50 for each part, while the cost to my readers was less than 1/3 the printed price. Further, I receive a considerably larger percentage of the gross – or about 3x what I was making per book.

> Considering those figures, why isn't every author writing eBooks?!
>
> Read the previous paragraph carefully; I said I make more per book ... I didn't say I sell more books.
>
> In moving from the world of the mega-publisher to the smaller world of self-publishing, you'll lose the marketing resources of the mega-publisher. The trade-off then, is more profit for fewer books sold. If you can handle the marketing, you can potentially make more than you could with the mega-publisher. (This idea works wonderfully if you're a teacher/professor who can require your own book.)

Finally, there's the reader. Tired? Can't find your reading glasses? Kids asking you to read to them when the Playboy channel is airing an interesting, uh, documentary?

Both the Adobe and Microsoft Readers come with a fancy tool that quite literally reads the book to you. The voice selection is limited, and Microsoft doesn't quite have all the inflections perfected yet (although they do a remarkable job), but you might find it nice to relax while someone reads to you for a change!

> Text-to-Speech became available with Windows XP. It may not work for earlier releases of Windows, but the download site is:
>
> http://www.microsoft.com/msagent/downloads/user.asp#tts

Despite all these wonderful pluses, eBooks do have their downside. First, although it's a growing market, it's also a new market; not everyone uses eBooks yet. You might not want to assume thousands of sales right out of the starting gate. Additionally, *an electronic book doesn't preclude the need for some sort of marketing plan.*

Security is also an issue. With the advent of CD-Rs, DVD-Rs, and computers that can copy just about anything, you might want to consider locking up your book somehow.

Most of the methods for applying security to a CD are expensive and unreliable – the same holds true for eBooks. You may also have to deal with the issue of providing your readers with a master copy of your book that can be printed any number of times. Of course, you won't get paid for the "any number of times" it's printed.

Adobe provides the best approach for dealing with both problems in its Content Server package. Unfortunately, this package costs about $5000 (plus the training required to operate it!). That'll bust the budget of any but the larger publishing houses. Luckily, other options present themselves. (There's always someone who takes the course and invests the bucks who's willing to sell his or her expertise ... sometimes even for a reasonable amount of money!) We'll discuss these options later, too.

Why not just go with the POD then?

Many people do. Many more use both.

EBooks require very little investment to create and produce. PODs require much more. Plus, as you'll soon discover, PODs are not as readily marketable as one might suppose. Bookstores actually place them behind the old vanity press books in desirability! Of course, bookstores have no way to market an eBook at all!

Step 1.4 — What Can I Expect Once I Create My eBook, Who's Going to Read It?

Simply put, the potential market includes anyone who reads.

Your reader will probably be young. That said, your author (me) passed the age of consent so long ago he's forgotten what it was that needed his consent in the first place! Most everyone is "young" to me!

Your reader will probably be somewhere between childhood (eBooks make great fun for the computer literate child) and his or her mid forties. Of course, he (or she) will also have some savvy in the world of technology.

The schoolbook/textbook market is crying to happen! What student wouldn't prefer a $10 book to a $100 book? What student wouldn't prefer carrying a 4.9oz reader that fits in a pocket (or even a single laptop or tablet computer) rather than five or six 10 pound textbooks? Additionally, folks who travel on business often have to carry a laptop or a PDA/Pocket PC anyway – why burden themselves with the weight of a novel to boot?

At this point in time, you can expect the market to continue growing – hopefully along with the desire of people to read your books.

Most of this information holds true for PODs, as well. However, the reasons might not be as obvious.

Bookstores don't (or rarely) carry PODs. Most of your POD sales, then, will come from online sources (Amazon.com and similar retailers). So your POD readers will also be computer and Internet savvy.

The similarities break down, unfortunately, when you consider that the eBook market holds great growth potential. The POD market, while growing, doesn't have the same potential as the eBook market.

Step 1.4 Summary

So now you know something about eBooks and PODs. You should notice a small crack in the well-entrenched seams of the book-world to which you've grown accustomed. Hopefully, your mind's gears have begun to churn as they formulate the beginnings of new possibilities ...

Let the mental gears roil while, in our next lesson, you get some hands-on experience using eBooks and the most popular readers available.

Following is a list of expenses associated with Lesson 1. I encourage you to invest in the Pocket PC as soon as possible.

Expenses Associated with this Lesson

Item	Expense (USD)		
	Min	Suggested	Max
Pocket PC	0	300	500+

Lesson

Following this lesson, you will:

- ✓ *Be familiar with the basic eBook reader applications*
  - ○ *Adobe Reader*
  - ○ *Microsoft Reader*
- ✓ *Be prepared to select which format(s) you wish to use*

Selecting a Format

In your training, you first worked to develop an understanding of eBooks – what are they, why should you create them, what can you expect from them, and so forth. The next thing you should do – the Second Step – is to decide which format(s) to use. Although many exist, only a couple show any potential for surviving the competitive nature of software design.

Let's take a look.

Step 2.1   I've Heard There Are Many Formats for eBooks, which Should I Use?

Many companies have produced their own reading software. Unfortunately, each reader application (software) requires that the eBook be created specifically for it. The good news (sort of) is that you don't have to produce your eBook in several formats – most of the formats won't last. Several have already disappeared.

Many of the handheld devices made by the larger companies (Dell, Hewlett-Packard, and others), as well as many PCs, often ship with one (or both) of two readers – *Adobe* or *Microsoft*. Both readers are free and both reflow text to make reading on a handheld device more convenient.

We'll concentrate our efforts in this book on those two readers.

You can download the free creation tool for Microsoft Reader (called *Read In*) from their website[2].

To create an Adobe Reader file (PDF), you'll need Adobe Acrobat (either the Standard[3] edition, which sells for about $299 or the Professional[4] edition, which sells for about $449). Alternately, Adobe provides a web-based subscriber service[5] for about $10/month that you can also use to create your PDFs.

Several considerations may affect your choice of eBook creation programs. Let's take a look at these.

- **Cost** – If you're self-publishing, this consideration may override all others. After all, nothing quite compares with *free*! But before you opt for the Microsoft approach, consider the $10/month web-based subscriber service[6] offered by Adobe. Although not without its limitations, this service makes it simple and inexpensive to convert your document for use by the most popular document reader around.

- **Target Platform** – Which operating system will you target?

    Microsoft holds most of the market here, so most of your potential readers will be able to use the Microsoft Reader. Apple hasn't yet produced an operating system for a handheld (well, not a successful one anyway), so that market won't be a problem.

    But what about Macs and Mac laptops?

    Microsoft Reader won't help you there.

    On the other hand, an Adobe PDF is a trans-platform format – it doesn't care if it's being read on a Mac or a PC. (Now you know why it's the most popular document handler around.) Adobe, then, has a wider platform target.

- **Graphics, Lists, Tables, and Text Boxes** – Microsoft Reader handled the graphics for my children's stories fairly well. It took some manipulation to get them properly located, but they looked good in the end. I found Adobe's handheld device interface (for Acrobat Reader) distracting for the children's stories until I put it in full-screen mode. The Adobe Reader interface, however, looked okay on my laptop and PC.

    > In the past, Adobe provided two readers – the newer version, Adobe Reader, worked well on PCs and laptops. Handheld devices, however, didn't have the resources to make the Adobe Reader work, so Adobe provided the older Acrobat Reader for them.
    >
    > Today, most handheld devices operate with version 2.0 of the Adobe Reader. You can download it from Adobe's website[7]. (Just identify your system, and

> Adobe will download the appropriate software.)
>
> We'll look at both the current reader (Adobe Reader 7) and the current reader for handhelds (Adobe Reader 2) in this text.

The place that Adobe really outshone Microsoft was in my AutoCAD textbooks. These are graphics intense (thousands of images) and contain dozens of tables and bulleted lists. By eliminating the tags when I created the PDF (more on tags in Lesson 3), I could limit the reflowing of text and keep the graphics exactly where I wanted them. Additionally, the Microsoft Reader just doesn't do bulleted lists (and isn't happy with tables). On the downside, without the tags, I found it impossible (well, really difficult anyway) to read these books on a handheld device.

- **Training** – This doesn't have to be a major consideration; both applications have a manageable learning curve.

Learning to use the Microsoft Reader creation program actually requires no training at all. Once you've installed it, simply pick a button and Microsoft will do the rest. You won't have many decisions (options) to make.

Adobe, on the other hand, has several books available to help you learn how to use it. You probably won't find it difficult (although you *will* face a steeper learning curve with the latest release – 7), but there are some options that make the reader's experience more enjoyable.

Speaking of which, let's look at the ...

- **Potential Reader Experience** – Readers like interactive ~~toys~~ (oops) tools – the more expensive they are, the more interactive they want them to be.

> When considering the potential reader experience with a specific reading application (in this case, Microsoft or Adobe Reader), always remember your target platform. Both applications offer options and opportunities on a PC that your reader won't find on a handheld device.
>
> I've found it wise to limit targeting handheld devices to my fiction books. Reading for enjoyment doesn't require

> much highlighting, listing, or column writing (unless you're my mother – Hickory – who, like me, can't read without a pencil in her hand).
>
> Textbooks, on the other hand, require both and are much more likely to use complicated graphics, lists, tables, and text boxes. I usually target PCs and laptops for that type of writing; the bigger machines allow my readers more application options.

With both readers, you can open and read a document. If you're on a handheld device and reopen it later, it'll open to the page at which it was located when you closed it. The readers can also adjust the text size – a very useful ability – and Microsoft Reader renumbers the pages accordingly. (Adobe Reader doesn't renumber pages.) Both readers also allow links within the document; this lets you set up a table of contents that allows the reader to pick a chapter title or heading and jump to it. Both also provide some sort of text-to-speech capability (although not on a handheld device). In fact, they use the same speech engine, so voices loaded for one will work for the other as well.

> Although a wonderful tool, some authors choose not to allow text-to-speech functionality in their books. The choice will be yours when you select someone to distribute and provide security for your book. But that's getting ahead of ourselves; we'll discuss security in more detail in Lesson 3.

Microsoft Reader allows the insertion of bookmarks and/or notes into a document; Adobe Reader does not. Microsoft Reader even allows the reader to circle or highlight selected text, as though he were reading with a highlighter in his hand. These extremely useful tools convince many people to opt for the less expensive Microsoft Reader.

Both applications will also allow the reader to search a document for specific text – a must for a student or instructor, especially when the document lacks an index. (In fact, such ability replaces the *need* for an index!)

Depending on the operating system, both will even allow the reader to landscape the screen for better viewing. (That is, you can rotate the eBook on the screen of a handheld device to see it better.)

Of course, the program size of Adobe Reader is considerably greater than Microsoft Reader's, and Acrobat Reader's user interface can appear cluttered on a handheld device (something that creates a nuisance in inverse proportion to the size of the screen on which the reader is working).

Download

With web access, Adobe Reader allows you to look for definitions of selected words. Microsoft Reader also allows you to look up definitions, but it doesn't require web access for its dictionary.

You will, however, need to download a dictionary before you can use it in the Microsoft Reader. Find it at Microsoft's dictionary download site[8].

Perhaps the biggest selling point in favor of Adobe Reader (besides its superior handling of tables and graphics) is simply that you, the creator, can edit the document after you've created it. Microsoft Reader requires that you perform any editing in the parent application (the one you used to create your book). Then you have to recreate the Microsoft Reader file. That editing ability in Adobe Reader, together with its popularity in the marketplace (it was the first application to do what it does), makes it a safe bet for those who can afford the creation software.

(Unfortunately, you won't find this editing ability in Adobe's Online tool.)

You won't need either Microsoft Read In or Adobe Acrobat to create your manuscript if you intend to produce just a POD. Most of the POD houses will accept MS Word or even Corel WordPerfect documents.

16

The following chart should help summarize this section for you.

Ability	Microsoft Reader	Adobe Reader
Allow text search	Yes	Yes
Allows highlighting, bookmarking	Yes	No
Conversion Application	Microsoft Read In	Adobe Acrobat
Conversion Application Cost	Free	$10/mo - $449
Conversion Application Training	Not Required	Available
Cost	Free	Free
Dictionary	Downloadable	With Web access
Editable	No	With Adobe Acrobat
Handling of graphics, lists, tables, text boxes	Poor	Good
Reflow and resize text	Yes	When setup properly
Target Platform (Operating System)	Windows	Most OSs
Training	Provided here	Provided here

Step 2.2 What Will My Readers Experience With These Applications?

This might be a good time to get our hands dirty. Let's take a look at what your reader will experience with these software applications. (We just want to get a feel for them.) For a more detailed 70 page course in Microsoft Reader, select **Help** from its main screen (see the first figure in the next exercise); for a handy 113 page instructional manual for Adobe Reader, go to: Adobe Reader User's Guide[9].

17

	Before you attempt these exercises, you'll need to download a couple sample files from: http://www.foragerpub.com/eBookFiles.
 Download	Look for two files – *Pirates.pdf* (an Adobe Reader file) and *Pirates.lit* (a Microsoft Reader file). Right-click on each of these files and select **Save Target As** from the popup menu. Save the files into a convenient folder (I put them in the *My Documents* folder because it's easy to find them). You'll also need to download and install both readers. Download the Adobe Reader from: Adobe.com[10]; download the Microsoft Reader from: Microsoft.com[11]. Follow the on-screen instructions for each.

Do This: 2.2.1	Get Familiar with Microsoft Reader

I. Be sure you have installed the latest version of Microsoft Reader.

II. Be sure you have downloaded the files mentioned in the above insert. When you installed Microsoft Reader, it created a directory called My Library in you're My Documents folder. Move the *Pirates.lit* file you downloaded into that directory.

III. We'll open the *Pirates.lit* file and take a look at the Microsoft Reader user interface. Follow these steps.

TOOLS	STEPS
 Microsoft Reader Desktop Shortcut	1. Open Microsoft Reader. It should have placed a shortcut on your desktop like the one shown. If not, follow this path: *Start – Program (or All Programs) – Microsoft Reader* (On a handheld device, follow this path: *Start – Microsoft Reader*.)

18

TOOLS	STEPS
	The Microsoft Reader looks something like the following figure.
The list of available books will depend on which books you've downloaded. If you have several, the *Pirates Beneath the Pavement* title may appear last – Microsoft Reader lists the books by date of access – the most recently opened appearing first on the list.

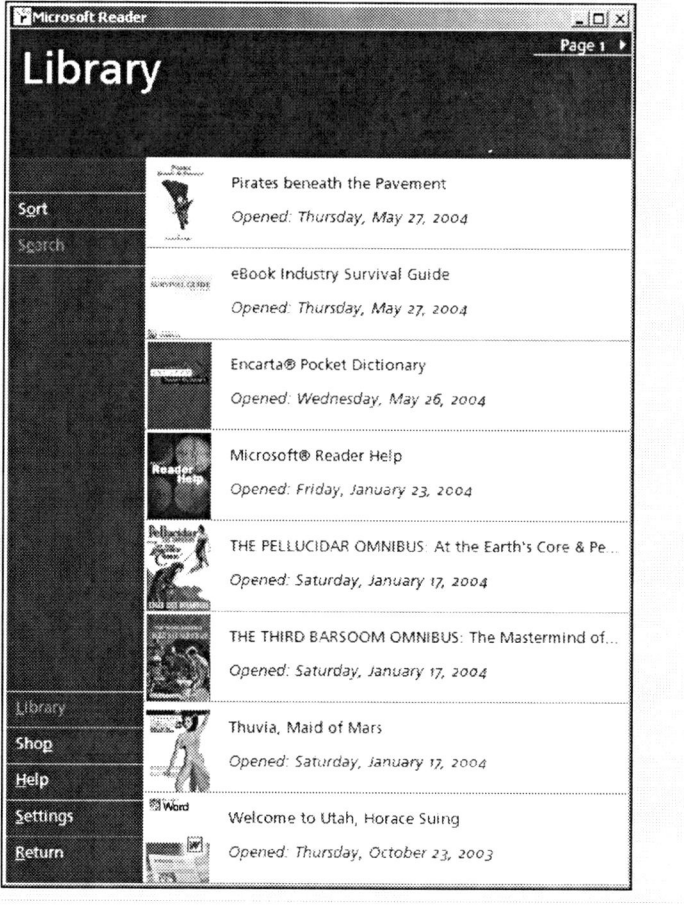

19

TOOLS	STEPS

In the red area down the left side of the Microsoft Reader window, you'll notice several options.

- **Sort** allows you to resort the list of titles by way of a popup menu. You can sort the list by **Title**, **Author**, **Last Read**, **Book Size**, and **Date Acquired**.
- Microsoft Reader makes the **Search** option available when you've sorted your eBooks by title or author. Use it to search for a specific title or author.
- The **Library** option becomes available when you're in **Settings** mode. It returns you to the library page (previous page).
- **Shop** provides two links – the first takes you to the Microsoft Reader website where you'll find a list of outlets that sell eBooks; the second takes you to a site where you can activate your reader. (We'll discuss reader activation in our next section.)
- **Help** allows you to search through the *Microsoft Reader Help* eBook for specific information. You'll find everything you need to know for operating Microsoft Reader here.
- **Settings** opens a screen where you can optimize the text size that Microsoft Reader uses to display your eBook. This comes in particularly handy on handheld devices!
- **Return** takes you back to the last thing you viewed in Microsoft Reader.

You can page through an extensive library using the **Page** numbering link found in the upper right corner of the reader.

The most prominent part the reader (when opened to the **Library** page) is the book list. Here you'll find titles, cover images, and a date indicating the last time you opened this title.

	2. Pick anywhere in the *Pirates Beneath the Pavement* frame to open the book.

20

TOOLS	STEPS
	Microsoft Reader briefly displays the book's cover image (something you'll design) and then displays the book's cover page (see the figure on the next page). Don't confuse this with the title page of the book; the cover page is still a Microsoft Reader screen.
	(It may take a few moments for a book to open for the first time on a handheld device because of the limited resources – RAM – found there.)
	Notice that most of the options remain in the red column. Microsoft Reader has paused to allow you to select another book (essentially, you've taken the book off the shelf, but you haven't really opened it yet).

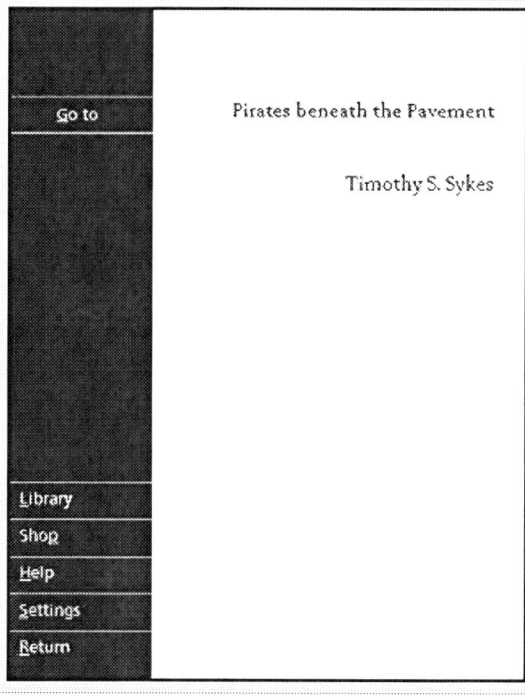

21

TOOLS	STEPS
	3. Pick on either the title or the author's name to open the book. (Alternately, you can use the **Page Down** key on your keyboard.) The reader opens the book (following figure).

Pirates beneath the Pavement

Pirates Beneath the Pavement

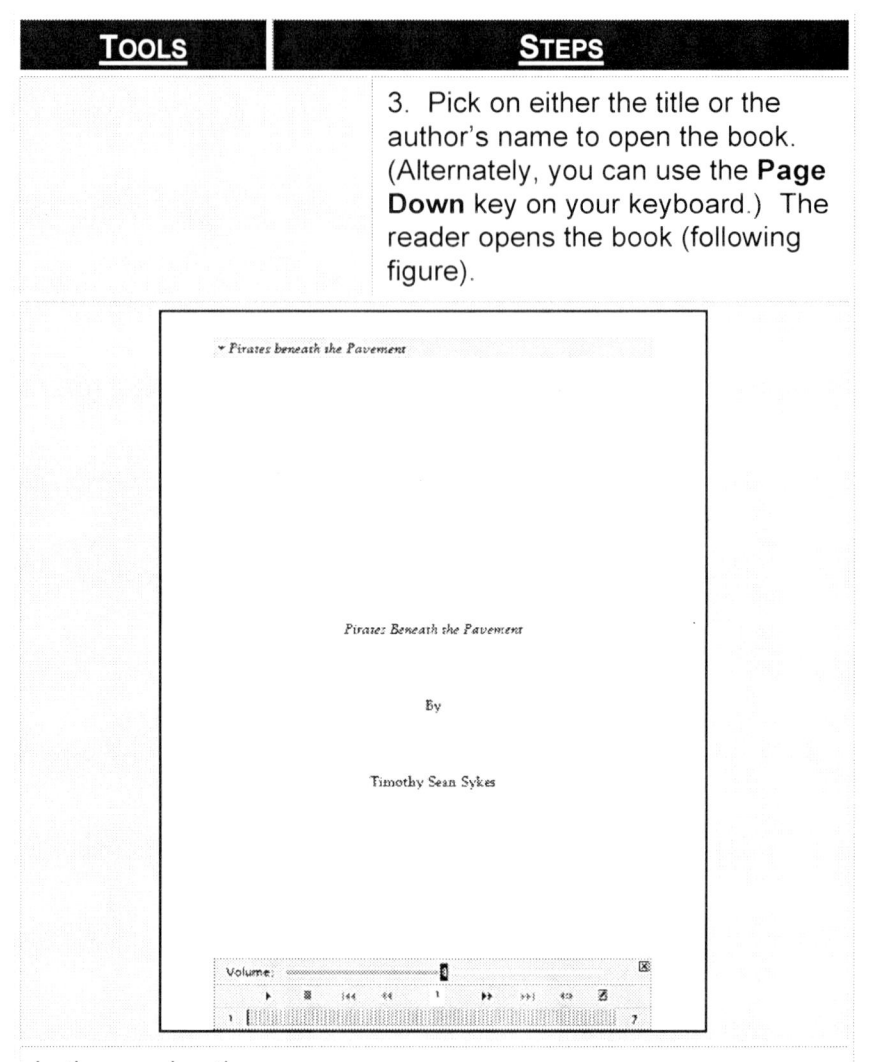

By

Timothy Sean Sykes

Let's examine the screen now.
- At the top, you'll find a Title Menu (the eBook title), which produces a popup navigation menu when selected. This menu provides options to:
    o Return to the **Cover Page** or the **Table of Contents**.
    o Display a list of **Annotations** associated with this eBook (picking on an annotation will transport you

TOOLS	STEPS

   to its location in the eBook and open the note for reading).
   - Open Microsoft Reader's **Help** book.
   - Return to the **Library** page.
   - Change the font **Settings** from within the eBook.
   - **Return** to the previous display (annotations list, opened book, etc.).
- The Text Display Area (below the Title Menu) covers most of the window. Here you see the title page of our eBook.
- Below the Text Display Area, you'll find the *Riffle Control*. This oddly named gizmo serves a dual purpose – it begins/ends the text to speech tool on a PC (your handheld device won't have these options), and it serves as a navigational aid. From the top, you'll find a volume control slider bar, navigational button bar, and navigational slider bar. The buttons on the navigational button bar are (from the left as shown in the last figure):
   - **Play** [not available on handheld devices] activates the text-to-speech tool; speech begins where the cursor was last located in the body of the text and continues until you push the **Stop** button.
   - **Stop** [not available on handheld devices] deactivates the text-to-speech tool.
   - **Section Back** – moves the display to the preceding section or to the front of the text if the publisher didn't use sections.
   - **Page Back** – moves the display to the preceding page.
   - **Page Number** – displays the number of the current page (this is not a hard and fast number; that is, Microsoft Reader repaginates when you enlarge or reduce the font settings; the current number of pages required for the eBook is shown to the right

TOOLS	STEPS
	of the navigational slider bar); you can display the Riffle Control by right-clicking on the page number (hide it by picking on the "X" in the upper right corner). o **Page Forward** – moves the display to the next page. o **Section Forward** – moves the display to the next section or to the end of the text if the publisher didn't use sections. o **Skip Ahead** – skips to the next section. o **Annotate** – creates a bookmark on the currently displayed page.
	Two other opportunities exist for navigating a document: the keyboard and a wheeled mouse. Use the keyboard's **Page Up**, **Page Down**, **Arrow Left**, and **Arrow Right** keys to move from one page to the next/previous. Use the **Home** and **End** keys to go to the beginning or end of the eBook. Use the wheel on the mouse to scroll from one page to the next/previous.
	4. Take a few minutes to experiment with the navigational controls and the text-to-speech tools. (If you don't have TTS tools on your PC version of Microsoft Reader, you can download it from TTS[12].)

Tools	Steps
Add Boo<u>k</u>mark Add <u>H</u>ighlight Add <u>T</u>ext Note Add Dra<u>w</u>ing <u>F</u>ind... <u>C</u>opy Text <u>P</u>lay <u>L</u>ookup...	5. Now right-click on any word within the document. Microsoft Reader displays the popup menu shown in the left column. Let's look at the possibilities. • Selecting **Add Bookmark** places a triangular bookmark to the right of the text. Picking this bookmark from anywhere else in the text will return you to the displayed page. The bookmark remains with the book when it is closed, so you can reopen to the marked page at any time. Additionally, it displays as a hollow mark on any but the marked page. Pick on the solid bookmark (it's solid when on the marked page) and select **Delete** from the popup menu to remove it. • Use pick-and-drag to select text in the document. (When you release the mouse button, the popup menu will automatically display.) Select **Add Highlight** to highlight the selected text. • **Add Text Note** will display a note box where you can enter any notes you might normally place in the margins of your book. The note box disappears when you pick anywhere else on the page. To review your note(s), you can pick on the note icon on the page or select **Annotations** from the Title Menu. • **Add Drawing** enables you to draw

TOOLS	STEPS
	lines or circles on the page. A Done/Undo toolbar appears at the bottom of the page when **Add Drawing** is in use. You must pick **Done** to exit the tool. (Use the box between **Done** and **Undo** to change the color of the pencil marks.)
	• To use the **Find** tool, first select some text. Find will then search the document for additional occurrences of the selected text. You can also enter another word to look for in the top of the search box.
	• **Copy Text** copies the selected text to the Windows clipboard. You can then insert it into another application. (Certain security options can disable this ability. More on that in Lesson 3.)
	• **Play**, of course, activates the text-to-speech tools.
	• The **Lookup** option appears only if you've downloaded and installed the Microsoft Reader dictionary[13]. If available, Microsoft Reader will look up the selected word in the dictionary for you. It will display the results in a popup window like the one seen in the figure following Step 10 of this exercise.

TOOLS	STEPS
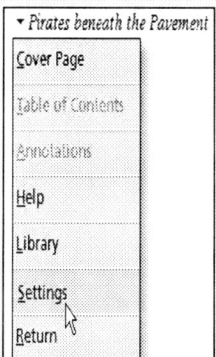	6. Now that we're familiar with the interface, let's see some of these tools in action. First, notice the number of pages shown to the right of the Riffle Control. Then pick on the title and select **Settings** from the popup menu (as shown). Microsoft Reader displays the font settings screen (following figure). Notice that the red column bar reappears and that Microsoft Reader makes a **Select Font Size** slider bar available. Below the slider bar, Microsoft Reader presents some text, which changes dynamically when you use the slider bar, to help you judge how large you want the font to be.

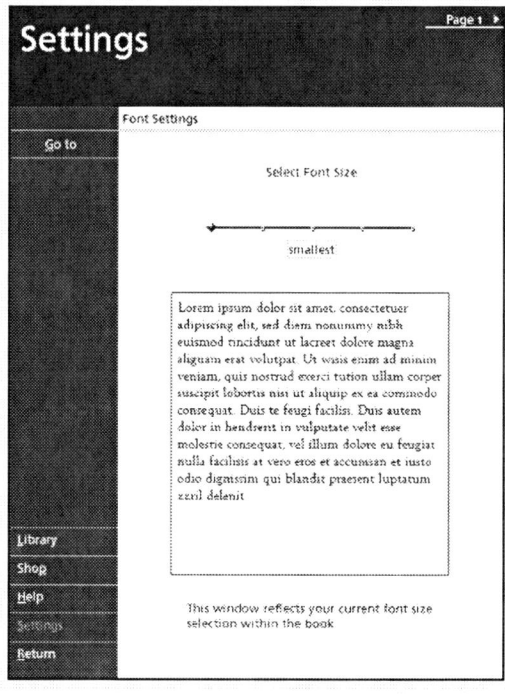

27

TOOLS	STEPS
Select Font Size / small	7. Slide the slider bar to the location one slot right of the left end of the line as shown (**small**).
Return	8. Pick **Return** to return to the *Pirates* eBook. Notice the difference in the font size and the number of pages in the eBook.
	9. Scroll to page 5 where you should find the image of little Rachel on a slide. If this image doesn't appear on page 5, keep scrolling until you find it. (Screen resolution may affect the number of pages and location of certain items within the Microsoft eBook.)
Lookup...	10. Right-click on the word "whimpering" and select **Lookup** from the popup menu; the word lies about three or four lines below the image. (If the menu doesn't have the option, you haven't downloaded and installed the dictionary. If you wish to do this before proceeding, go to this site: Microsoft Reader Dictionary[14].)
	Microsoft Reader presents a popup window with the selected word and its definition (figure – next page). (Isn't that handy!)
	You can enter another word in the space where you see "whimpering" and pick **Lookup** (to the right) if you'd like to look up something else.
	Pick anywhere else on the page to close the dictionary.

TOOLS	STEPS
	Encarta® Pocket Dictionary whimpering　　　　　　　　　　*Lookup...* **whimper** *v* 　1. sob softly 　2. complain peevishly 　3. say something plaintively *n* 　1. whine 　2. complaint
Add Bookmark	11. Let's place a bookmark. Right click on the first word in the paragraph above Rachel and her slide, and select **Add Bookmark** from the popup menu. Notice the solid red arrow that appears in the right margin of the page.
	12. Scroll through another few pages. Notice that the arrow becomes an outline.
Delete Change Color	13. Pick on the arrow's outline. Microsoft Reader returns you to the page with Rachel's image! (Right-click on the arrow and pick **Delete** from the popup menu to remove the bookmark. Microsoft Reader will ask if you really want to delete it; pick **Yes** from the available options.) You can add or remove as many bookmarks as you'd like. Microsoft Reader will place them in a column down the right margin.

TOOLS	STEPS
	14. Now we'll highlight some text. Holding down your left mouse button, drag your cursor over the paragraph below the image. Notice that you've selected the paragraph. (Don't worry if you can't select the entire paragraph.)
	15. Release your mouse button. Notice that a popup menu appears.
Add Highlight	16. Select **Add Highlight** from the menu. Microsoft Reader highlights the selection as though you'd used a yellow marker! As with the bookmark, the highlighting will remain when you close the text, so you can refer to it again later.
Edit Highlight	17. Let's remove the highlighting. Reselect the text. When you release the mouse key, you'll notice that the **Add Highlight** option has changed to **Edit Highlight**. Select that one. A new popup menu appears.
Erase	18. You can change the color of the highlighting (to help you organize your notes), or you can erase it. Select **Erase**.
Add Text Note	19. You can select images as well as text. Pick on Rachel's picture. Notice that you get the same popup menu. Let's add a note – select **Add Text Note**. Microsoft Reader presents a note box (following figure).

Image #3 - Rachel on a slide.

30

Tools	Steps
	20. Enter the text shown, and pick anywhere outside the text box to close it. Notice that Microsoft Reader places a note icon (it looks like a piece of paper) next to the image.
📄	21. Pick on the note icon to reopen and read the note.
Delete "?"	22. Again, pick outside the note box to close it. To delete it, right-click on the icon and select **Delete** from the popup menu. Microsoft Reader will prompt with a "Do you really want to" box; pick **Yes**.
Find...	23. The **Add Drawing** option on the popup menu works just like the **Add Text Note** and **Add Highlight** options, so let's move on to the **Find** option. Right-click on any occurrence of the name "Rachel" and select **Find** from the popup menu.
	Microsoft Reader presents a search box (following figure) telling you the object of the search (in this case, *Rachel*) and allowing you to look for the **First** occurrence, the **Previous** occurrence, or the **Next** occurrence. You can also restrict your search to an **exact match** or an **approximate match** (such as *Rachel's*).
	Rachel Find First Find Previous Find Next ▼ Use exact match

31

Tools	Steps
	24. When the search box is open, you can also enter another word you'd like to find. Try entering "pirate" and picking the **Find First** option. Notice that Microsoft Reader takes you to the appropriate page and highlights the word. Why didn't it take you to the word "pirates" on the title page?*
☒	25. Pick the exit button (**X**) in the upper right corner to close the Microsoft Reader.

You can see that a printed text doesn't give you much in the way of utility that you can't get with Microsoft Reader. (I suppose you could use the pages of a printed book to start a fire in the woods if you were lost, but how often does *that* happen?!) And the best news about Microsoft Reader – the interface changes very little between the PC version and the handheld! (Handheld devices don't allow for text-to-speech; otherwise, you won't find any difference!)

But remember, Microsoft's is not the most popular reader! Let's take a look at the Adobe Reader.

Unfortunately, you'll soon discover that Adobe Reader doesn't share Microsoft Reader's user-friendly interface. Additionally (and more unfortunately), Adobe Reader's interface on a handheld device differs radically from its PC sibling. Still, Adobe Reader's pan-system architecture helps it maintain its popularity.

(What the %$#@ is *pan system architecture*? Don't fret; that's just a fancy way of saying that a Mac user can use Adobe Reader the same way a PC user can.)

Since you have no way of knowing which tool (PC or handheld device) your readers will use, we'll take a look at both interfaces.

---

* You're doing an exact match search; to find approximate matches, pick the arrow next to **Use exact match** and select the appropriate option.

(If you don't have a handheld device yet, just review that section for now.)

We'll use the *Pirates.pdf* file you've already downloaded (or will download). Why, you may wonder, will we use a file other than the one you already have opened (this text)?

Well, this text appears in two formats – eBook (which most of you will be using) and good old fashioned printed book (POD). Those who use the printed version will need a file to view; those who are using the eBook have already opened the Adobe Reader. You're getting familiar as you go (but you can still go through the following exercise using this text instead of *Pirates*).

| Do This: 2.2.2 | Get Familiar with Adobe Reader – PC Version |

I. Be sure you have installed the latest version of Adobe Reader.

II. Be sure you have downloaded the *Pirates.pdf* file (http://www.foragerpub.com/eBookFiles). Place the file in your My Documents folder.

III. We'll open the *Pirates.pdf* file and take a look at the Adobe Reader user interface. Follow these steps. (Readers using the eBook text can skip Steps 1 and 2 and use the eBook rather than *Pirates.pdf*.)

TOOLS	STEPS
Adobe Reader 7.0	1. Open Adobe Reader. It should have placed a shortcut on your desktop like the one shown. If not, follow this path: *Start – Program (or All Programs) – Adobe Reader*
	2. Pick the **Open** button on the File toolbar (just below the File pull down menu). Adobe Reader uses a Windows standard open dialog box, which defaults to the My

33

TOOLS	STEPS
	Documents folder. Select the *Pirates.pdf* and pick the **Open** button in the dialog box. Adobe Reader opens the file (below). (You screen may look different depending on the size of your Adobe Reader window.)

Adobe Reader - [Pirates.pdf]
File Edit View Document Tools Window Help
48%
Bookmarks
Pages
Attachments
Comments
Pirates
Beneath the Pavement
by
Timothy Sean Sykes
1 of 12

	3. Let's pause to examine the user interface.

As you can see, the Adobe Reader interface appears quite a bit busier than Microsoft Reader's. But Adobe Reader provides more options, too. Let's start at the top.

- Adobe Reader has a typical pull down menu system just below the title bar. Most of the options beneath each heading are typical of Microsoft applications. Some notable exceptions include:
    - Perhaps the most important tool you'll find in the pull down menus lies beneath Files. Here you'll find the tool needed to activate your reader for purchased eBooks. Follow this path: **Files – Digital Editions – Authorize Devices**. Here you can activate the DRM for your reader. (DRM – Digital Rights Manager – it's what prevents readers from copying your books and passing them around.) You needed to activate your manager to read the eBook version of this text, so you may already be familiar with this tool. You'll need internet access, a few minutes (faster connections mean fewer minutes), and a (free) .NET passport, but it won't cost you anything. Just follow the instructions.
    - *Adobe's Digital Media store*[15] where you can shop for new and exciting eBooks. You'll find access to this handy link by following this path: **File – Digital Editions – Adobe Digital Media Store**. Here you'll find a list of eBook providers.

> The *Adobe Digital Media store*[16] quite naturally lists only sellers of eBooks in the PDF format. Other popular sites sell both the Adobe format and the Microsoft format. These might help you get started in your shopping experience:
>
> Amazon.com[17] (primary retailer of all sorts of books – often offers discounts); Powells.com[18] (up-and-coming book retailer – good discounts); Fictionwise.com[19]; eBooks.com[20].
>
> Additionally, quite a few sites are available which offer free eBooks (ebookdirectory.com[21]), but I recommend approaching them with caution. *Free* is

> a wonderful concept, but it's been my experience that few things require as much work as something that's free!

- A **Read Out Loud** option beneath the View heading (I suppose they couldn't find a logical place for it); this correlates to the same option in the Microsoft Reader. Unfortunately, this is the only place you'll find this option, so toggling **Play – Pause – Stop** can be a chore.
- The Document's pull down menu contains options for checking **Digital Signatures** and **Digital IDs**, as well as inspecting attachments to the PDF and checking accessibility. These options provide some security for corporate secrets, but they're not much use to an eBook writer.
- Toolbar buttons provide better ways to access most of the options of the Tools pull down menu. Using the **Basic** option under the Tools pull down menu, you'll find several tools repeated on the Basic toolbar. These include:
    - **Hand Tool** – turns the cursor into a hand; when active, you can use the hand to scroll through the pages of your book (pick and hold the left mouse button while dragging the pages of your book up or down, or side to side).
    - **Select Text** – changes the cursor to an I-Beam; drag this over text to select it for copying to the clipboard. (This assumes the eBook's security settings permit you to copy text to the clipboard.)
    - **Snapshot Tool** – changes your cursor to crosshairs; but you can use these crosshairs to window around a section of the document (pick and drag with the left mouse button). Adobe Reader then places the text or images within the window as an image on the clipboard.

- Below the pull down menus, Adobe Reader provides ten toolbars. (Toggle these on and off by right-clicking on an open toolbar and selecting a toolbar to turn on/off.) These include:

Toolbar	Buttons (from left)
File Toolbar	**Open**, **Save As**, **Print**, **Send as Email**, **Search**
Basic Toolbar	**Hand tool**, **Select tool** (for selecting text), **Snapshot tool**
Zoom Toolbar	**Zoom In** (flyouts to **Zoom Out** and **Dynamic Zoom**), **Fit Page**, **Fit Width**, **Zoom Out**, **Zoom** (display and manual set), **Zoom In**
Rotate View Toolbar	**Rotate Clockwise** (flyout to **Rotate Counterclockwise**)
Edit Toolbar	**Spell Check** comments and forms, **Undo** (flyout to **Redo**), **Copy**
Navigation Toolbar (not in default display)	**First Page**, **Previous Page**, **Next Page**, **Last Page**, **Previous View**, **Next View**
Find Toolbar	**Find** (flyout to options: **Whole Word**, **Case-Sensitive**, **Bookmarks**, **Comments**), **Find** text box, **Find Previous** (occurrence), **Find Next**
Object Data Toolbar	**Object Data Tool** (for use with some CAD-produced PDFs)

Toolbar	Buttons (from left)
[search box] Y! Search the Web Toolbar	**Yahoo Search** engine for your web browser

We've already seen explanations for most of these tools, but some others merit your attention.

- Three buttons on the Zoom toolbar will prove themselves quite useful, although easily forgotten. The **Fit Page** and **Fit Width** buttons instantly adjust the size of your page in Adobe's window.
- You'll probably not find rotating a page useful very often – in fact, you can remove the **Rotate View** toolbar to allow for more viewing room if you prefer. (Then again, I've landscaped a page before for a better fit – this can make viewing these pages easier!)
- Spell checking works only for comments and field entries. If you need to spell check the document otherwise, you'll need to do it in the source document before you create the PDF (or in Adobe Acrobat).
- **Find** satisfies the need for an index. Rather than search an index, simply search the document with this tool.
- Use the **Object Data Tool** to provide information about graphics created by Microsoft Visio.

- Down the left side of the Adobe Reader, you'll find several tabs. (There are actually seven Navigation tabs. Access them by following this path: **View – Navigation Tabs – [tab]**.) These produce *navigation panes* (columns) to help you move through the document.
  - The **Bookmarks** tab displays quick links to any bookmarks in the document, including the Table of Contents. Pick on any bookmark to navigate to the page that contains it.
  - The **Signatures** tab displays the digital signatures of anyone who has altered or commented on the

document. Business people find this more useful than eBook readers.
- The **Layers** tab enables you to toggle layers in documents created with Microsoft Visio drawings. Like signatures, this information has more of a business use; eBook readers probably won't need this tab.
- The **Pages** tab displays thumbnail images of all the pages in the eBook. Use the scroll bar in the navigation pane to move forward or backward in the book, and select a page to display it in the document pane (the reading window).
- An Article weaves its way through a document in much the same way a newspaper article appears on multiple pages. Using the **Articles** tab, you can open an article attached to a PDF and easily follow it through the document.
- Sometimes, you'll find a PDF has a non-PDF document attached to it. Use the **Attachments** tab to locate and open these. This can be a useful tool for textbook creators who wish to provide source documentation.
- **Model Tree** can be useful for files containing elements created with Adobe Acrobat 3D. This very expensive tool is beyond the scope of this text. If, however, you intend to create an eBook or PDF that takes advantage of some of the elements of a 3D CAD package, you might look into this application.

- Below the document pane, you'll find the primary navigation tools. These are identical to those found on the navigation toolbar, with a few additions.
  - The **Page Number Display** does just that. You can also enter a page number here to go directly to that page.
  - The last four buttons (right) include:

    Last Four Navigation Buttons

    - **Single Page** – sets the document pane to view a single page at a time.

39

- **Continuous Page** – sets the document pane so that you can scroll from one page to the next without "jumping" between pages.
- **Continuous - Facing** – sets the document pane so that you can scroll facing pages.
- **Facing** – sets the document pane so that you can view two pages at one time.

- Not busy enough yet? There's more! The Adobe Reader also provides a right-click cursor menu (right).

    Right-Click (Cursor) Menu

    o In the first frame, you can access the zoom tools available on the Zoom toolbar, or you can tell Adobe to **Allow Hand Tool to Select Text**. This convenient features means you won't have to use the **Select Tool** to select text. (Adobe automatically changes to the I-beam cursor when you pick on a word.

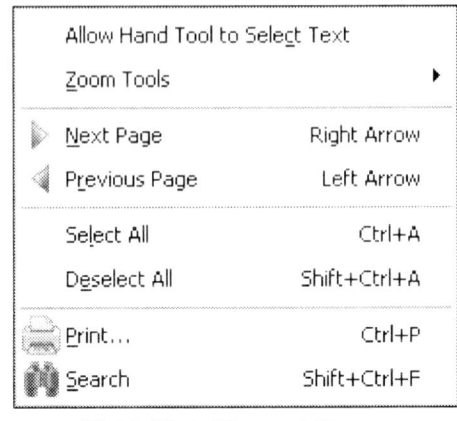

    o The second frame provides redundant navigation options– **Next Page** and **Previous Page** – for your convenience.

    o The third frame allows you to **Select** or **Deselect** the entire document for copying to the clipboard. (These options may not be available depending on the author's security choices.) The selection will include text but not graphics.

    o The final frame provides these options:
        - **Print** – calls a print dialog box (this option may be disabled by security settings).

- **Search** – like the Microsoft Reader **Search** tool, this enables you to search the eBook for specific text. The Adobe Reader version of **Search** has a friendlier user interface, is more familiar to Windows users (oddly enough), and has more user-defined parameters.
  - You'll find another convenient feature when you right-click on a selected word. In addition to a couple **Copy** options and the same **Select** options found in the previous

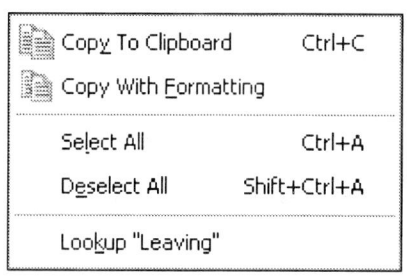

Copy To Clipboard	Ctrl+C
Copy With Formatting	
Select All	Ctrl+A
Deselect All	Shift+Ctrl+A
Lookup "Leaving"	

    Cursor Menu when Right-Clicking on a Selected Word

    menu, now you have a **Lookup** option for the selected word. It works something like its counterpart in the Microsoft Reader. Unfortunately, the Adobe Reader version requires an internet connection (it uses a web-based dictionary). Previously, Adobe used a bad dictionary (I can say that now – it's been replaced!) Now it uses *Dictionary.com* – a reliable and reputable tool.

Now that you've had a look at the Adobe Reader interface, let's continue our exercise (Do This 2.2.2) and experiment with some of the possibilities.

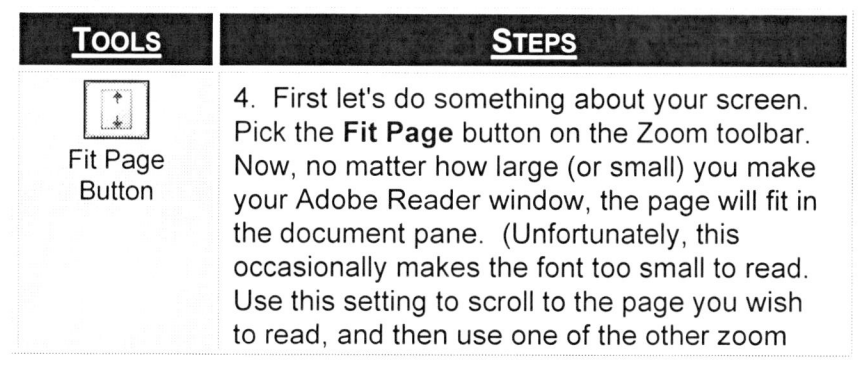

TOOLS	STEPS
Fit Page Button	4. First let's do something about your screen. Pick the **Fit Page** button on the Zoom toolbar. Now, no matter how large (or small) you make your Adobe Reader window, the page will fit in the document pane. (Unfortunately, this occasionally makes the font too small to read. Use this setting to scroll to the page you wish to read, and then use one of the other zoom

TOOLS	STEPS
	options for better text viewing.)
	5. Use the wheel on your mouse to scroll down a page or two. (Those of you without a wheeled mouse can skip this step.)
	Does Adobe Reader display a couple pages at a time? We can fix that.
Single Page Button Continuous Button	6. Pick the **Single Page** button (on the status bar) and repeat Step 5. Notice that the Adobe Reader scrolls pages rather than lines on a page. Use this setup to move through the pages faster; use the **Continuous** button (to the right of the **Single Page** button) to scroll as you did in Step 5.
Next Page Button Previous Page Button	7. Use the **Next Page** and **Previous Page** buttons to scroll through the pages. (You'll find these both on the status bar and on the right-click cursor menu.) Notice that these scroll full pages regardless of the **Single Page/Continuous** setting.
First Page Button	8. Now go to the beginning of the eBook by picking the **First Page** button (to the left of the **Previous Page** button on the status bar).
6	9. Enter a page number in the **Page Number** box (between the **Next Page** and **Previous Page** buttons). Use the **Enter** key on your keyboard to move to that page.
Previous View Button	10. Now use the **Previous View** button to return to the last page (the first page of the document).

TOOLS	STEPS
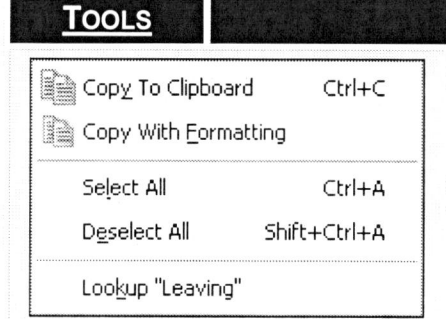 Copy To Clipboard Ctrl+C Copy With Formatting Select All Ctrl+A Deselect All Shift+Ctrl+A Lookup "Leaving"	11. You can see that the Adobe Reader makes it easy enough to navigate pages. Let's take a look at some of the other tools. Right-click on a word (any word will do – as long as it's text and not an image), and select **Look up** ... from the popup menu. Your browser should open to the *dictionary.com* site and display a definition of the selected word.
	12. Close the browser and any popup windows.
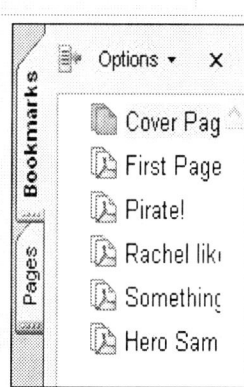 Options ▾ x Cover Pag First Page Pirate! Rachel lik Something Hero Sam	13. Adobe Reader also handles bookmarks differently from Microsoft Reader. Pick on the **Bookmarks** tab to the left of the document frame. A bookmark frame appears as shown (if you're using this text rather than Pirates, you're bookmarks will be different). (If your list disappears in the right hand column, select **Wrap Long Bookmarks** from the **Options** drop down menu.) Look around the bookmarks pane. Select a bookmark or two – they'll take you to a page (or image in this case) just as the Microsoft Reader did. Bookmark descriptions make it a bit easier to know which bookmark to select in Adobe Reader. (That's the good part.) Unfortunately, *the reader can't add his/her own bookmark!* (You knew there had to be a downside, didn't you?)

TOOLS	STEPS
	Remember then, if you opt to build an eBook using the Adobe format, you might be generous with your bookmarks. (On the other hand, bookmarks increase the size of the file; if you're too generous, your file becomes too large for some retailers to handle. You may find yourself forced to distribute your eBook on a CD. Costs go up ... security becomes an issue ... profits go down.)
	14. Pick on the **Bookmarks** tab again to close the Bookmarks Pane.
Search Button	15. Let's try a word search. Pick the **Search** button on the toolbar. Notice that a search pane appears to the right of the document pane. You have a few more options here than in most Windows search panes (**Search the current PDF**, search **All PDFs in My Documents**, etc.), but the basic search tool is the same used in most Windows applications.
	16. Be sure there's a bullet next to **In the current PDF document**, and enter some text in the **What word or phrase would you like to search for** text box. (*Pirates* readers enter "pirate"; text readers enter "Adobe".)
Search	17. Pick the **Search** button to continue. Adobe Reader lists links to the locations of the target word (next page). You can pick on a link to move to that page.

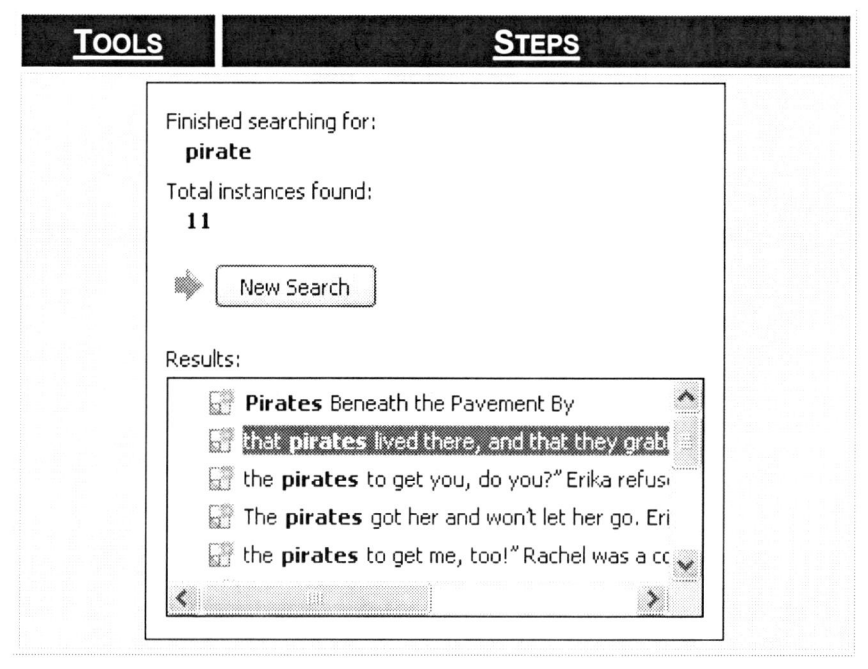

TOOLS	STEPS

	Finished searching for:
	  pirate
	Total instances found:
	  11
	➡ [New Search]
	Results:
	  📄 **Pirates** Beneath the Pavement By
	  📄 that **pirates** lived there, and that they grab
	  📄 the **pirates** to get you, do you?" Erika refus
	  📄 The **pirates** got her and won't let her go. Eri
	  📄 the **pirates** to get me, too!" Rachel was a cc

Adobe Reader shares Microsoft Reader's ability to select and copy text (you can use the Edit pull down menu's **Copy** command, right-click popup menu, or Windows standard keyboard approach to copy selected items to the clipboard). In some ways, such as better zoom tools, Adobe Reader offers some improved capabilities. But as you've seen, the Adobe Reader has some definite disadvantages – it doesn't allow the reader to change the document in any appreciable way (you can't add bookmarks ... or notes), the user interface requires a greater learning curve (more time for a reader to become comfortable with it), and some tools require Internet access.

> Adobe does allow the reader to place bookmarks, comments, notes, etc. in their PDFs if the reader uses either the Standard or Professional editions of Adobe Acrobat. But most readers won't want to make the investment required for such privileges.

Your readers may find one other characteristic of the Adobe Reader to be something of a disadvantage – it has a radically different user interface when used on a handheld device.

Let's take a look at this interface. (If you don't have a handheld device, read over this material to get a feel for what your readers will find.)

Do This: 2.2.3	Get Familiar with Adobe Reader – Pocket PC Version

    I. Be sure you've installed the latest version of Adobe Reader. (I'm using Adobe Reader 2.0 for handhelds.)

   II. Be sure you've downloaded the *Pirates.pdf* file (http://www.foragerpub.com/eBookFiles). Follow the instructions that came with your device to transfer the file to it.

  III. Follow these steps. (All readers should use the *Pirates.pdf* file; while the text is readable on a handheld device, tables – such as the Do This exercises – and some graphics don't always translate well.)

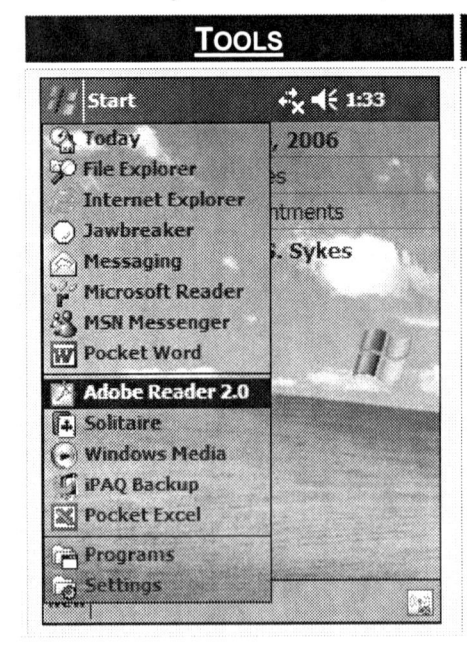

TOOLS	STEPS
[screenshot of Pocket PC Start menu showing: Today, File Explorer, Internet Explorer, Jawbreaker, Messaging, Microsoft Reader, MSN Messenger, Pocket Word, **Adobe Reader 2.0**, Solitaire, Windows Media, iPAQ Backup, Pocket Excel, Programs, Settings]	1. Open Adobe Reader. Follow this path as shown: *Start – Acrobat Reader* (If the Adobe Reader doesn't appear under the **Start** button, it may be because Windows for a Pocket PC doesn't allow unlimited program listings. Check with the device's documentation to see how to list the Adobe Reader.)

46

TOOLS	STEPS
Acrobat Reader Open Screen	2. Adobe Reader presents an Open screen, which lists the PDFs available on the device. Select the *Pirates* file. (You'll select with a stylus on your Pocket PC by touching it to an image or piece of text.) The reader will open the file.
Adobe Reader User Interface	3. The Adobe Reader screen appears with the **Pirates** ebook open. (If it doesn't look exactly like this, don't worry. We'll look at the interface now.)

Starting from the top, you see the:

- Title bar – picking on the title will open the Windows Start menu. Picking the **X** to the right of the title bar will remove the reader from the screen. (You can turn the reader application off by selecting **Exit** from the Document Menu – more on this in Step 8.)

47

TOOLS	STEPS
• Navigation Pane Toggle line (a pair of arrows pointing up/down) – this opens the navigation pane (more on that in a moment). • Document Pane – for viewing the document; this pane contains standard scrolling bars for navigating the document. • Toolbar – contains single pick navigation, viewing, and document options. Navigation Pane	4. Open the Navigation Pane (shown here) by picking the up/down arrow bar above the Document Pane, or by picking the up/down arrow button on the toolbar.

The Navigation Pane resembles its namesake in the Adobe Reader for PCs, except that you haven't as many tabs. Pick on a tab to open it. Pick on any listing in any of these tabs to display that page in the Document Pane.

- **Articles** – displays connections for multi-page articles like those that might appear in a newspaper or magazine. Most eBooks don't need article threads.
- **Bookmarks** – displays the same information you found on the **Bookmarks** tab in the PC version. Try picking on some of the bookmarks. Notice that you move to the appropriate page. Don't worry if the text suddenly shrinks – the reflow is toggling off. You'll see how to toggle it back on in Step 5.
- **Pages** – displays the same information you found on the **Pages** tab in the PC version. Try picking (double-click) on a page or two and notice how the screen changes to the appropriate page.

TOOLS	STEPS
Full Screen Reflow Automatically Scroll Go Back Go Forward Default Zoom Zoom In Zoom Out ✓ Hand Tool Text Select Tool Zoom-in Tool Copy Select Current Page	5. Pick and hold with your stylus anywhere in the Document Pane to display the View menu (shown here).

Most of the options are fairly clear.

- **Full Screen** – removes the title bar, scroll bars, and toolbars. This makes for a less cluttered display and often a more enjoyable reading experience. To redisplay these items, pick and hold anywhere in the Document Pane and remove the check next to the **Full Screen** option. Try this now.
- **Reflow** – toggles reflow mode on and off. This can help when viewing a document with tables. Toggle this off to see the effect, and then toggle it back on.
- **Automatically Scroll** – causes the screen to automatically scroll. You have to be a fast reader to keep up with this!
- **Go Back** and **Go Forward** – takes you to your previous view or returns you to your current view (as the **Previous View** and **Next View** buttons do in the PC version).
- **Default Zoom**, **Zoom In**, and **Zoom Out** – standard zoom controls. With **Reflow** toggled on, these can increase/decrease text size for easier viewing.

TOOLS	STEPS
• **Hand Tool** – enables you to move the document "page" about the screen by dragging your stylus over it. Try this now; then toggle **Reflow** off and try it again. Do you see how convenient this can be when looking at a page that doesn't reflow? (Toggle the **Reflow** option back on.) • **Copy** becomes available when you select a word or **Select Current Page** – this copies the selected material to the clipboard.	

You can pick in any open area of the Document Pane to close the View Menu.

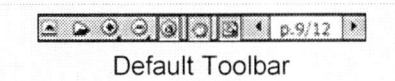

Default Toolbar	6. Look at the toolbar. It presents several options.

These are (from the left):

- **Document Menu** button – more on the Document Menu in Step 7.
- **Open Document** button – calls the Open screen shown in Step 2.
- **Zoom In** and **Zoom Out** buttons – increase or decrease the area of the screen (makes the text larger or smaller).
- **Default Zoom** button – returns the screen to the default magnification (you can set the default on the Preferences screen –discussed later in this exercise).
- **Hand Tool** button – enables you to move the page by dragging the stylus around on your screen.
- **Reflow** button – toggles reflow on or off.
- **Previous Page** – places the previous page in the display.
- **Page Indicator/Go To Page** – use this to locate yourself within the eBook. Try this: pick in the page frame. Acrobat Reader will present a keyboard image on the screen (see the figure below). Enter a page

TOOLS	STEPS
number and pick the **Enter** key to move to that page. • **Next Page** –places the next page in the display.	
[on-screen keyboard image]	
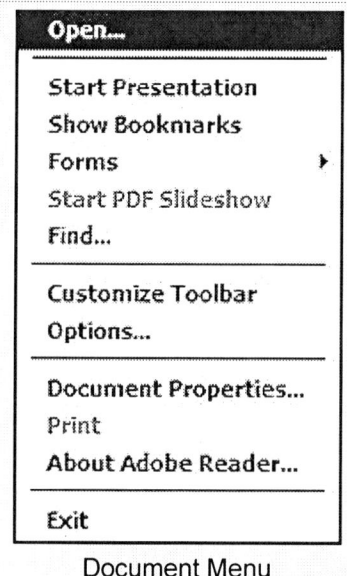 **Open...** Start Presentation Show Bookmarks Forms ▶ Start PDF Slideshow Find... Customize Toolbar Options... Document Properties... Print About Adobe Reader... Exit Document Menu	7. Pick the **Document Menu** button on the toolbar. Adobe Reader presents the Document Menu shown here.

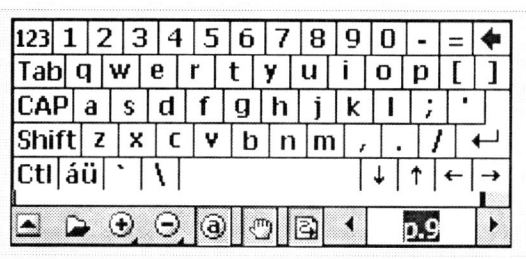

- **Open** – presents the Open screen we discussed in Step 2.
- **Start Presentation** – starts a slideshow. You must have a VGA graphics card for this to work.
- **Show Bookmarks** – displays the Navigation Pane we discussed earlier. Adobe Reader will place the **Bookmarks** tab on top.
- **Forms** – gives you the opportunity to use forms in your PDF (not a common need for eBooks). This pick offers

51

TOOLS	STEPS

several options: **Import** or **Export Forms Data**, **Submit Offline Data**, or **Mail Forms Data**.

- **Start PDF Slideshow** – begins a slideshow if one has been created.
- **Find** – presents a Find dialog box. We'll look at this in Step 8.
- **Customize Toolbar** – presents a list of buttons available for the toolbar (across the bottom of the screen). Bear in mind that you can only have ten buttons (depending on which buttons you select). Add or remove the ones you want.
- **Options** – opens an Options screen. We'll look at this in Step 17.
- **Document Properties** – presents information about the currently open document (see the following figure). As the author, your readers will expect you to enter the information in the text boxes when you create the PDF. Adobe will gather the rest of the information when it creates the file.
- **Print** – lets you to print if your handheld has the capability and the security has been set to allow it.
- **About Adobe Reader** – presents a screen of patents, author, legal, and trademark information.
- **Exit** – stops the application. (Note: The Microsoft Reader has no such option. When you pick the title bar's **X**, Windows removes the application from the screen, but you'll need to follow a procedure to actually shut it off. Look in your devices operating manual for details on this procedure.)

TOOLS	STEPS
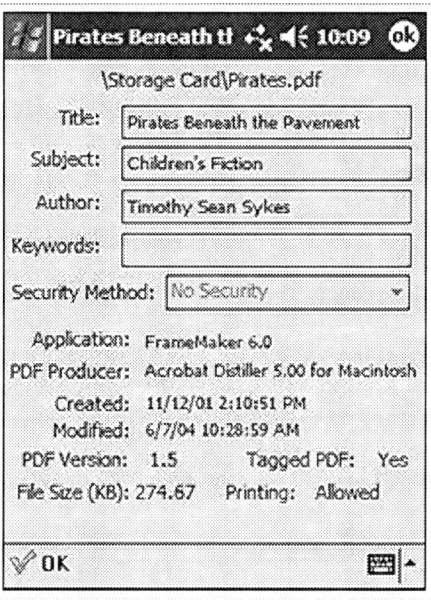 (Document properties dialog showing Pirates Beneath the Pavement PDF metadata)	
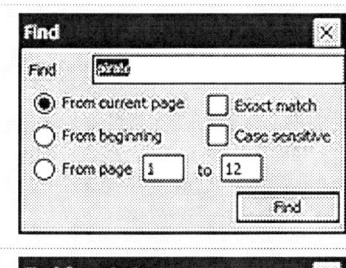 (Find dialog box with "pirate" entered)	8. Pick the **Find** option on the Document Menu. Adobe Reader presents a find dialog box (shown). 9. Enter *pirate*, as shown, and pick the **Find** button.
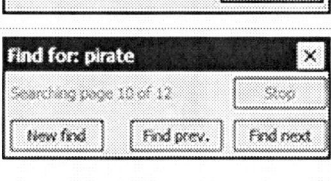 (Find for: pirate dialog, Searching page 10 of 12)	10. Adobe displays the page where it finds the entry, highlights the entry, and asks if you'd like to continue your search for other occurrences. Pick the **X** on the title bar to close the dialog box.

53

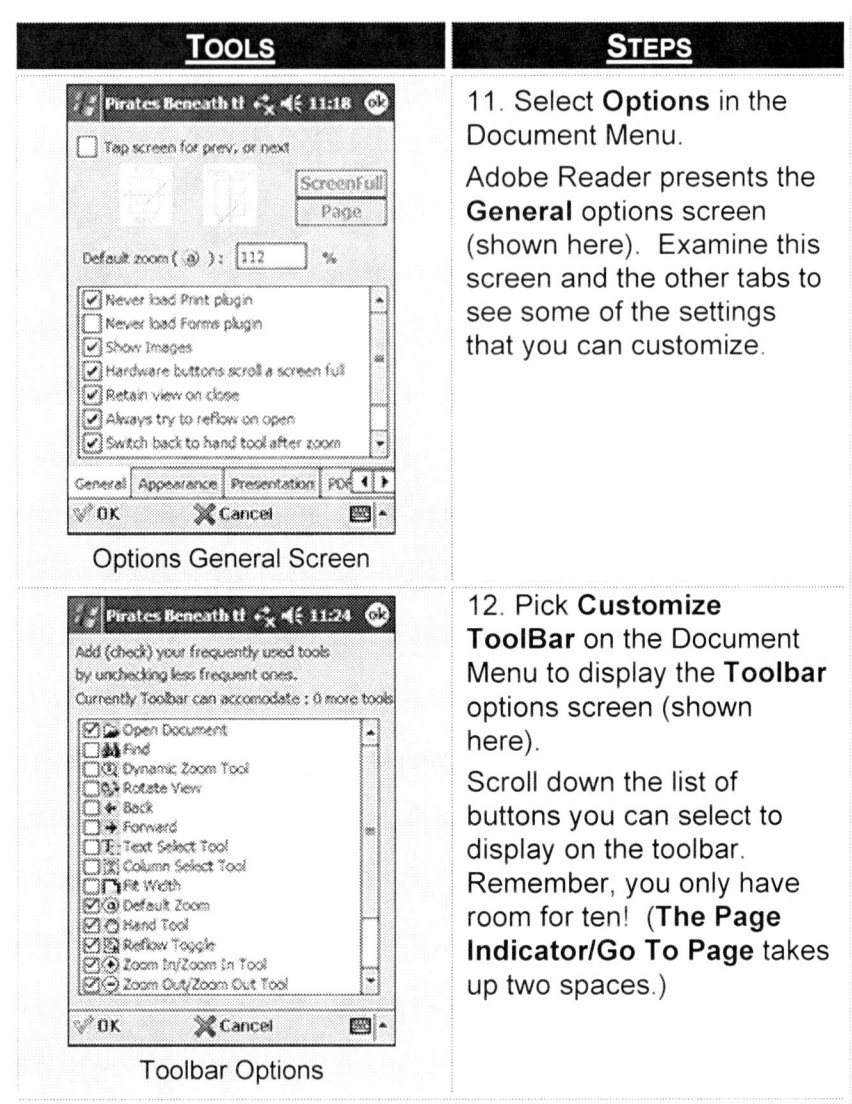

TOOLS	STEPS
Options General Screen	11. Select **Options** in the Document Menu. Adobe Reader presents the **General** options screen (shown here). Examine this screen and the other tabs to see some of the settings that you can customize.
Toolbar Options	12. Pick **Customize ToolBar** on the Document Menu to display the **Toolbar** options screen (shown here). Scroll down the list of buttons you can select to display on the toolbar. Remember, you only have room for ten! (**The Page Indicator/Go To Page** takes up two spaces.)

Try this: remove the check from the **Default Zoom** option. Notice that the other buttons become available. Place a check next to **Fit Width** and pick the **OK** button to complete the procedure.

Notice that the **Default Zoom** button disappears from the toolbar and a **Fit Width** button appears.

Pick the **Fit Width** button. Notice the change in the display.

Tools	Steps
This handy tool makes viewing tables much easier! (Microsoft Reader doesn't have this option either!) Pick the **Reflow** button to return to the previous display.	

For more on the Adobe Reader's capabilities refer to the *User's Guide* that ships with it.

That was a lengthy answer to the last question – *I've Heard There Are Many Formats for eBooks, Which Should I Use?* But without familiarity with the most popular readers, an author/publisher will have a difficult time providing a product his or her readers will enjoy.

You have some other considerations when determining the format for your new eBook. Let's look at those now.

Step 2.3 — **What About Security – I Don't Want People to Steal My Work?**

Neither application (Microsoft Reader or Adobe/Acrobat Reader) wins prizes for their approach to security. Both make it possible to prevent theft, but you need to involve some sort of publishing house with access to the proper software (or shell out the $5000 for Adobe's Content Server). Microsoft Reader doesn't allow printing of a document for any reason; you can, however, control whether or not a reader can print a PDF, and you can control the quality of the printing allowed. (You can control it by number of pages allowed in a given time frame with Content Server.)

Adobe also allows you to put passwords on a file controlling who can open it. But let's face it, a buyer has to have the password, or he'll want his money back. Once he has the password, he can as easily pass it on to someone else as he can the eBook itself. So password-protecting the opening of an eBook won't do you much good – and it'll probably irritate your readers. Adobe does, however, allow you to insert a password protecting printing options and content copy options.

Although not strictly a concern when selecting which application to use, distribution goals have a direct effect on security. If you intend to distribute your own eBooks (via your website or CD) *and you don't have access to Content Server*, the last few paragraphs detail the limits of the security availability to you. If, however, you intend to go with a POD/eBook publisher (such as Lightning Source[22], AuthorHouse[23], Xlibris[24], iUniverse[25], or others), you'll have other security options. First among these is that any eBook purchased through these sources will require an *activated* reader and will lock the purchased eBook to that reader. This effectively stops any sharing of your eBook.

We'll discuss security in more detail in Lesson 5.

Before you go overboard on the security front (and become an eBook Rambo), you might want to consider your position in the book market. You can spend hundreds of dollars to list your eBooks with a POD publisher (except for Lightning Source – but we'll talk about them in more detail later). They'll promise you the sun and the moon – at a price. In the end, you'll have a book that sells for ten or twenty dollars (you'll get a couple dollars from each), and you'll have to sell hundreds of books to break even. Unless you already have a name in the field in which you're writing (such as a professor who can require his or her own text), you're not likely to have much success without spending hundreds more on marketing.

If you're prolific (you write many children's books or something else with a large volume of production), you might consider releasing the first two or three books without security.

Will they be copied and passed around? If you're lucky. But everyone who reads them will also learn your name ... and hopefully search out other works you've created. You can put security on those!

Step 2.4 Summary

As you've seen, the type of book you've written will, in large part, determine the reading application you'll want to use. Fiction converts to Microsoft Reader quite easily and without expense. Nonfiction with or without some graphics, but without tables and bulleted lists, also converts easily. You'll want to convert your nonfiction containing tables or lists to the Adobe format.

Both formats provide a functional, even enjoyable, reader experience when you (the author) use the correct reader. Neither requires much of a learning curve beyond what you've read here, so your reader should be able to begin reading your eBook almost as soon as the download is complete!

Many POD houses or publishers will convert your book for you ... at a price. Alternately, you can save some money and do it yourself. Of course, you'll need some experience in doing the conversion. You'll have this once you've completed Lesson 3!

Following is a list of expenses associated with Lesson 2.

Expenses Associated with this Lesson

Item	Expense (USD)		
	Min	Suggested	Max
Microsoft Reader	0	0	0
Adobe Reader	0	0	0
Adobe Security – Content Server	0	0	5000+
Microsoft Security	0	0	0

Lesson 3

Following this lesson, you will:

- ✓ Know what you need to produce an eBook
  - o Production Software (Adobe vs. Microsoft)
  - o Word Processors
  - o Graphics and Illustration Tools
  - o Cover tools
- ✓ Know what you need to prepare for marketing an eBook
  - o Business stuff (Copyrights, LCNs, etc.)
  - o Websites
- ✓ Know about what self-publishing your book will cost

Gathering Your Tools

I have to warn you before you start this lesson, self-publishing isn't free ... and it isn't always cheap! You can cut some corners to shave some of the expense, but if you cut too many, you'll end up with a cheap product that people won't buy. If you go all out, on the other hand, and spend as if you own the bank, you may find yourself losing a ton of money.

This lesson will show you what you'll need to self-publish. You'll probably already have some of the applications and material you'll need. You may need to invest in others. I'll make some recommendations as we go, but I don't know your financial situation. So I'll get you started on this lesson with an adage: Work from your heart, but *think about what you spend!*

Step 3.1 | **What Will I Need To Produce My eBook or POD?**

You probably already have a pretty good idea of what you'll need, but there's nothing like a check list to help you organize your thoughts. (My wife often accuses me of being unable to do anything without first putting it on a list!)

- Of course you'll need a **Word Processor**. I'm afraid the old reliable Olivetti (typewriter to you younger folks) has seen its day. Everything nowadays has to have RAM and pixels and a mouse and other such things. (Hickory – the Irish tree frog – threatens to wash my mouth out with soap when I talk about those things!) But let's face it; without computers, you wouldn't be trying to learn about eBooks in the first place!

  You'll need one of two word processors – Microsoft's *Word* or Corel's *WordPerfect*.

    o Microsoft Word[26] enjoys user-friendly interfaces with the tools required to create eBooks (and PODs) for both Microsoft Reader and Adobe Reader. These interfaces mean a lot more to someone who's tried to create an eBook without them.

      The Adobe Acrobat interface becomes available when you install Adobe Acrobat Standard[27] or Professional[28] edition. The Microsoft Reader creator

> becomes available when you download[29] and install MS Read In. (Note: As of this writing, you can only use Microsoft Read In in the 2002 or 2003 versions of Word.)

If you're using Word but have no formal training in it, I strongly recommend one of those continuing education courses at the local community college or a Microsoft Training Center[30]. (Check around, many community colleges *are* Microsoft Training Centers.) You might be surprised at some of the things Word can do that you haven't discovered yet! Plus it gets you out of the house (writers are notorious cave-dwellers).

> Microsoft Word sells alone for about $229 ($109 for the upgrade)[31]. (Note: You can upgrade from most versions of the Microsoft Works Suite, which ships with most computers.) It's also a cornerstone of all of the Microsoft Office Suites[32].

- As far as document creation goes, I can't think of anything you can do with Word that you can't do with WordPerfect[33]. Unfortunately, the user-friendly tools available for creating eBooks in Word simply don't exist in WordPerfect. You can still produce a PDF – but you'll have to use Adobe's PDF converter (available in your printer selection when you install the Standard or Professional edition). You can't create a Microsoft Reader eBook from WordPerfect.

If you still opt for WordPerfect (some of us just hate changing word processors), the same suggestions hold for training. You may find it more difficult to find a Corel Training Partner[34], but many community colleges offer courses in WordPerfect.

> WordPerfect Office sells for about $299.[35]

Writers operating on an absolute shoestring budget can create their book in Microsoft **WordPad** or Microsoft **Notepad**. Both ship free with all Microsoft operating systems. You may not be able to save formatting information (bold, italics, fonts, etc.), but you can add this information from within Adobe Acrobat. (Of course, if you can afford Adobe Acrobat, you probably should invest in a word processor first.) I don't recommend this approach, as what you save in money eventually costs you in time and tedium.

> Most POD houses will accept .doc files, which both MS Word and WordPad create by default.

- You'll need the **creation software**.
  - If you don't have the Adobe Acrobat software and plan to get it, Adobe makes two versions – Standard and Professional. Standard works well for most eBooks. Professional allows you to add some bells and whistles that increase the file size but may make an eBook more attractive. Before you decide, consider the price difference ($299 for the Standard[36] and $449 for Professional[37] as of this writing) against how much profit you hope to make with your eBooks or PODs.

    Adobe provides a useful (and inexpensive) alternative in their web-based subscriber service[38], which allows you to use a web-based application for $9.99/month (or $99.99/year). I recommend using this for beginning writers/publishers who haven't a lot to invest up front.

    If you intend to produce the Adobe/Acrobat format, you'll need an understanding of the software. Pick up a copy of the *Adobe Acrobat Classroom in a Book*[39] (Adobe Press, $45.00 or generally less at Amazon.com) or *How to Do Everything with Adobe Acrobat*[40] (McGraw Hill, $24.99 or generally less at Amazon.com). If you have the software, be sure your book matches what you have! Radical changes sometimes occur between releases.
  - If you intend to use the Microsoft Reader application, you can download the free creation tool (MS Read In) from Microsoft's website.[41]

I recommend creating a Microsoft Reader file regardless of whether or not you create a PDF. (Bearing in mind, of course, Microsoft Reader's formatting restrictions already discussed.) After all, the creation tool doesn't cost you anything, and posting a Microsoft Reader formatted eBook doesn't require additional ISBNs when you go through Lightning Source.

- If you plan to use graphics and/or illustrations in your eBook or POD, you'll need an appropriate **Graphics Application** for obtaining and/or creating, sizing, and manipulating your graphics.

> Before using graphics (such as clipart) from an application, check the legal statement that accompanies the application. Most applications (like Microsoft Office products) allow you to use their clipart for noncommercial uses or websites. If you sell your eBook or POD, you cross the line into commercial uses so *don't use application clipart!*

Luckily, you have a few options. Let's look first at your options for acquiring graphics, and then we'll look at manipulating them.

> You might think that someone who makes his living as a draftsman/CAD (Computer Aided Designer) professional should be able to draw. Well, the truth is that I've never been able to draw a crooked line without a template (or a computer)! I was lucky enough, however, to live in a time when plastic templates and computers abound!
>
> Of course, I had no trouble creating AutoCAD graphics for my textbooks. But other graphics (such as the guy stretching the dollar that appears in this text) presented a problem. Read on to see how I solved it.

  o Clipart.com[42] provides commercial clipart at a reasonable price (from $9.95/week to $169.95/year for all you can use). With some careful planning, you can take the one week option. To do this, finish writing your eBook, decide where you'd like graphics, and then purchase/download your material from clipart.com.

OUCH!

I used to opt for the three month package and search for graphics as I write. But it cost less when I did (49.95 vs. 59.95 as of this writing). Today I opt for Curious Lab's (now e-Frontier's) Poser[43]. (More on that in a moment.)

You can adjust the images from clipart.com as you require, and they provide photographs, fonts, sounds, and web art, too. Still, it's a good idea to read the user's agreement here as well.

- Poser[44] is the next step in illustration – 3D Figure Design and Animation. I used it to illustrate *How to Fart Like a Lady*[45] (the only book I've written using a pseudonym). You'll need some real

Poser Creation

computer skills to use it, but the results will knock your socks off (see the sample)! The price - $249.99 as of this writing – can be prohibitive for someone intending only one book. So think before you buy.

Then again, once you buy, you'll want to invest in some of the pre-designed characters available from several third party sources (Daz3d.com[46] is by far the best and most reasonably priced, but Renderocity.com[47] runs a close second. Both provide several freebies!) The biggest problem you may have with Poser is the desire to play with it rather than work on your book!

- If you just can't find what you like, you can always hire a commercial artist to illustrate your book. But be warned, your checkbox may need therapy when you've finished. I haven't found a professional illustrator that didn't want my first born for his efforts.

I solved the problem with my second children's book (*F'Lump's Adventures Continue with Timmy and Tarbaby*) by posting an ad at several local colleges (on the Art Department bulletin boards) asking for someone willing to work for what I could afford (which wasn't much) and a byline on the cover. I met a talented young lady who needed the money to help with her education and recognized the benefit illustrating a children's book could provide to her résumé and experience.

Once you've acquired your graphics, you'll need to get them into your computer (if you've hired someone to create them) and get them ready for your book – that is, size (in terms of inches, centimeters, and so forth), file size, background transparency (if desired), and such things as brightness, contrast, and color.

- You'll find a very basic image manipulator in **Microsoft Paint**, which has shipped with Microsoft operating systems since the beginning. It's free; but unfortunately, you can't do much with it – some simple sizing and color manipulating, but that's about all.
- **Paintshop Pro**[48] comes from Corel (formerly from Jasc) and sells for about $99 (downloaded). Paintshop Pro provides just about everything you'll need for simple to fairly complex graphic manipulation.
- Adobe once again provides the high-end graphics production tool with its **Photoshop**[49]. As a rule, if Photoshop can't do it to a graphic, it probably can't be done. Unfortunately, its $649 price tag and its training requirements put it out of reach of most of us common folk.

Of course, there are dozens of other graphics programs on the market. I've given you just a few samples. But when making your choice, consider the following:

- **Cost** – can you recover the price (together with the rest of your investments) in your book's first year's sales?

When considering cost, the new self-publisher (as with anyone new to anything) will probably forget to figure something very important into his or her calculations. But it's easy to overlook (your calculator doesn't have a button for it).

It's very difficult to work *experience* into your number crunching. But don't underestimate its value. The fact is that your first book *may* ... indeed the odds are that it *will* lose money (at least initially). Although you can limit most of your initial investments to ouches rather than squeals, they do tend to add up. But don't forget to put experience in the plus column of your spreadsheet. Its cash value will present itself in time.

My best advice to first time writers is this:

> *Dream* of a bestseller,
>
> *Work* for a profit,
>
> *Hope* to break even, but
>
> *Expect* to lose money.

I don't say that to discourage you; far from it! My whole purpose in writing this text is to help you increase the odds of your initial success. But you can't win a battle if you don't know what you're up against.

That being said, you'll be surprised how much easier – and less expensive – your second effort will be!

- **Image Types Available** – few programs make all images available for your editing needs. Select one that can edit (at a minimum) JPGs, GIFs, BMPs, WMFs, and TIFs. When possible, use either JPGs or GIFs in your book. These provide the best quality files at manageable sizes. TIFs can also be very useful. (In the end, you'll even have to save your Poser characters in an image file.)
- **Manipulation Tools** – can you: adjust contrast and brightness, resize and crop, mirror, convert from one file type to another, work with photographs (remove

redeye, enhance colors, etc), change object colors easily, add text, and merge/join different graphics?

Of all the graphics programs on the market, I prefer Paintshop Pro for working pre-existing graphics into my books. It provides all the tools I need (and more), is reasonably priced (although on the outer edge of what I wanted to pay), and although the learning curve runs a bit steeper than I like, I learned how to use it in a reasonable amount of time. Corel provides a trial version[50] with tutorials (and special offers) that can help you make your final decision.

- Working along side your graphics applications, you'll need some additional **Cover Tools**. Luckily (and mercifully), these won't cost you anything. But you will need some technical information:
  o The sizing of your book (standard paperback sizes [in inches] include: 5 x 8, 5.5 x 8.5, 6 x 9, 6.14 x 9.21, 7.5 x 9.25, 7.44 x 9.69, 8.25 x 11, and 8.268x11.693; standard hard bound sizes include: 5.5 x 8.5, 6.14 x 9.21, and 6 x 9). You'll want to give your cover imaging about a 1/8" overhang for trimming.
  o The thickness of your book to at least 1/16" (go for 1/32" if you can get there). With LSI's tools, the number of pages will do.
  o The color requirements for your cover.
  o Cover copy. This critical paragraph or two may be the most difficult you'll ever write; but (or because) it'll go a long way toward selling your book. Readers browse for books by cover appearance first, then by what they read on the cover. (This information will also appear on your website and in the descriptive section of your book at Amazon and other POD and eBook seller sites.) Spend some time on this. It should be alluring, enticing, promising, and make a potential reader crave more! (But remember, you only have a paragraph or two!)
  o An artist's eye for creation and a reader's eye for what catches a book-shopper's attention.

I'll recommend two sources for tools to help you create your cover.

- If you intend to use one of the POD companies (AuthorHouse, Xlibris, iUniverse, etc.), they can create your cover for you ... or as much of the cover as you'd like. Bear in mind that the folks creating your cover probably won't read your book. They'll ask you some questions and work up something generic. (That said, their covers appear professional in every way, so don't let the "generic" aspect discourage you.) You can provide a cover graphic to help things along if you wish. (Refer to the previous Graphics Application section for help.)
- If you wish to create your own cover, I strongly recommend using the Book Designer's Resources at the Lightning Source website[51] (look under the Resources pull down menu). Here you'll find two tools – a Spine Calculator[52] to help you determine the thickness of your book (you'll need to provide the number of pages), and a Cover Template Creation Tool[53], which responds to your input with a full template you can use to create your cover (including ISBN number and bar code).

> Okay; this might be helpful for the PODs, but why would you need this information for an eBook?
>
> Well, remember that an eBook has to fit on the PC or handheld device's screen. Most of the standard book sizes work well for this, although the standard 8.5 x 11 sheet is pretty large. I like using the 8.5 x 11 sheet, but landscaping it and putting the text into columns. It fits a computer screen really well, and the columns break the text up for easier reading.
>
> If, however, I intend to create both a POD and an eBook, I size the book for the POD. It's easier to create an eBook from POD sizing than vice versa.
>
> As for the rest of the information, I recommend you browse amazon.com for eBooks[54]. You'll notice that

the first thing you see – even for eBooks – is a thumbnail image of the books' covers. (You'll also notice that Amazon carries thousands of eBooks with which you'll be competing.) So remember, even an eBook needs to catch the eye of a potential reader.

The front of your cover will also appear as the first thing your reader sees when he or she opens your eBook. So it's important to put some thought into its creation.

But what about all that sizing information? You can ignore it *only if you never plan to print your book!* Personally, I've never been willing to accept that the public won't line up in demanding lines for an autographed copy of one of my masterpieces! And even if eBooks pay the bills, you just can't sign the things! Besides, there will always be the diehard reader who simply demands something tangible. (I once fielded a reader complaint that he'd had to spend $19.90 for a 1400+ page textbook ... and I hadn't even "print[ed] or ship[ed] anything!" I guess he figured I'd written all those pages on a lark.)

So the second thing to remember here is to prepare for the future. Converting 1400+ pages to a printable format was a daunting task; it's better to set it up initially. Then if a market develops for a printed version of your book, you'll be ready.

Of course, I didn't mention talent for creation. You'll need some feel for what the actual graphic for your cover (if any) should look like. For this, you can consult that illustrator we discussed earlier, or you can work with one of your favorite graphics from inside the text. But if you walk the shelves at your local library or bookstore, you'll see that nothing is sacred (short of blatant pornography ... in most cases, anyway).

- Every writer (even the self-published) needs a good **Proofreader**. Treat your proofreader with love and respect, shower her with gifts and praise and appreciation.

(Okay, I've used my dear mother – the famous green, Irish tree frog, Hickory – since I began writing paragraphs back in fifth grade.) But insist that she demand utter and absolute perfection in your grammar and usage, and clarity in your style. She must be unmerciful in her demands if you are to succeed.

But she can follow her criticism with a nice cookie after she dustpans your remains from the floor.

Look for proofreaders in your local writers' guild or in a course at the local community college. But remember that other writers may not be as merciless as a proofreader should be. They know too well what it's like to be criticized. (This is where that thick skin develops in the writer.)

You're looking for someone that will approach your work in much the same way as your Senior English teacher did in high school (or even that %@$# graduate assistant in your college freshman course). You can also post a note on the local college's bulletin board (in the English department) for a student or grad student willing to work for a smile. There is no other place on Earth so packed with inexpensive talent as our local colleges!

Professional proofreaders do exist for those who can't find someone at a reasonable price. But be warned, the cost of a professional might be more than your book earns in a year! Here are some examples:

- Simply English Proofreading[55] offers many packages. The basic proofreading package begins at $3/page. (For a 300 page novel, that's $900! I'm afraid to calculate what my 1500+ page AutoCAD books would've cost.) OUCH!
- Creative Edge[56] offers fewer packages and higher prices – about $15-20/thousand words (that works out to as much as $5.00/page). (Their prices have recently risen – they cost less when we released the first edition of this text!)

- Finally, ACE Copyediting[57] offers the widest variety of packages, but charges an hourly rate that is harder to track or estimate. Their rate is $35/hour ($45/hour for technical writing).

There are other firms available (search the web to see the range). But this gives you some idea of what you're facing ... and incentive to support that English grad student!

> One quick note here: with the advent of spelling and grammar checkers in the modern computer word processor, you'll face the temptation of using them *instead of a human proofreader.* That's a **mistake**! These tools are helpful for high school students writing their term papers, but their usefulness to a professional writer are very limited! Use a real live person with real training!

Once you've found a proofreader that will work with you, remember two things – you must *listen* to them on all matters concerning the tools you've used to create your book (words, grammar, usage, etc.), so learn from every red mark they bleed onto your text. And once that's done, remember that *you have the last word on how your book is written.*

Having now written of the importance of a good proofreader, I must qualify my text with an admonition. Don't expect your proofreader to work from scratch! *Learn the tools of your trade before you write a book!* If you can't put two words together without murdering the language, please get some training first.

My old freshman English professor did me a world of good when he repeatedly stenciled those miserable words upon my papers – **GRAMMAR AND USAGE!** I hated him and those words, but I couldn't have become a writer (or passed his course) without learning the tools.

Step 3.2 What Will I Need To Market My eBook?

Having worked with publishers, I've discovered that they tend to believe marketing is a writer's job. While no one can speak about a book as well as the author, it seems that the publisher could take a proactive hand to earn the 85% to 95% of your book's gross that he's going to keep. (Where exactly are all those *contacts* they're supposed to have?)

That simple statement goes far to explain why writers like me have finally forgone the efforts required to convince someone else to publish our work. If I have to do the selling anyway, I may as well do the rest of the publishing process myself, too. (To this reclusive writer, selling requires work. The rest of the process just takes time.)

Much of what you'll need to market your book comes in the form of luck, stamina, self-assurance, desire, and fortitude. POD writers can always find addresses for bookstores. Unfortunately, they soon discover that bookstore chains assume POD means Pass, Overlook, and Disregard! To them, POD falls just below the old vanity press books (didn't know you could go lower, did you?). (In their defense, bookstores need to buy in volume to stack their shelves. They return the unsold books, and POD printers don't always accept returns.)

eBooks, on the other hand, don't require an author/publisher to beg someone else to sell their books; they simply have to let the world know where their books can be found via the Internet.

But regardless of how you sell your book (eBook or POD), you'll need some tools. Let's take a look at those.

- Depending upon whom you select to publish/distribute your eBook, you may need an **ISBN** and a **bar code**. (AuthorHouse, Xlibris, and iUniverse provide one; Lightning Source does not.)
    o An ISBN (International Standard Book Number) makes your book uniquely identifiable to a machine reader. Over 150 countries and territories officially use ISBNs, and you can't sell books in stores or through established retail outlets in the US without one. (Not

having one, however, will not stop you from selling your books through your own website or at country fairs.)

Many places offer ISBNs. Approach them with caution. LSI requires that your ISBN be registered to the publisher with whom they will be working. Your best bet is to go to Bowker.com.[58] You can buy ISBNs in batches of 10, 100, 1000, or 10,000. The current prices are: $225/10, $800/100, $1,200/1000, or $3,000/10,000. If you're only doing one book, you may want to opt for a POD publishing house. (But then, what writer plans to stop at one book?!)

The ISBN will go on the cover (with the bar code) and in the book's front matter (those pages that you usually ignore – with all that stuff about the publisher, disclaimers about the book being fiction, threats about making copies, and so forth.)

o You've probably seen **Bar Codes** – those odd stripes that they scan at the checkout counter of most stores in the US. These represent the ISBN of a book in a format that the machine can identify. (They represent other things for other items.)

Many applications exist that can create a bar code for you – but they all cost money. (If you decide to buy a software

Sample ISBN Bar Code

package that creates bar codes, be sure before you buy it that it will create ISBNs – they don't all do so.) Lightning Source offers some *free* tools that will benefit the self-publisher, including a bar code creator. Check out the **Resources** pull down menu at their website.[59]

(Use their Cover Template Creator – it includes a bar code.)

Once you've created your bar code, you'll need to save it in a graphic format that you can use – usually a gif or jpg. (Refer back to the sections on graphics and cover tools.) Save it to about a 2"W x 1"H image (measure a few on books you have around the house and use an exact measurement from one of them ... just to be safe). You can use one of many graphics programs we've already discussed to assist you.

On a printed book, the bar code goes on the back cover of the book and must be clearly readable through any shrink-wrapping or other packaging. You won't need one on an eBook. (You will, however, still require the ISBN.) You'll use an ISBN on a CD, as well; and the bar code should go on the back of the cover.

- A **Copyright** is a legal protection for authors of original literary, dramatic, musical, artistic and other intellectual works. Most writers won't face copyright problems, but not wishing to be the one who suffers at the hands of a nut with a lawyer, I always play it safe and follow the legal procedures.

  To officially copyright a book, send one printed copy (even if you'll publish it as an eBook; send two if the work has already been published), $30, and the appropriate form (short for most original, not-for-hire works by a single author,[60] standard[61] otherwise) to:

  > Library of Congress
  > Copyright Office - TX
  > 101 Independence Avenue, S.E.
  > Washington, D.C. 20559-6222

  For works created after March 1, 1989, you technically don't have to place a copyright notice in your work. Personally, I've always been too proud of mine to leave it out. Place the notice (consisting of the year of the copyright, followed by the copyright symbol - © - and finally by the name of the copyright owner, as in: 2004 ©

Timothy Sean Sykes) in an obvious place. Most publishers put it toward the bottom of the second or third page, and share the page with acknowledgements, LCCN data, and rights information. For more information on placing the copyright symbol, see the US Government Copyright Circular #3.[62]

For more information on copyrights, visit the US Government's Copyright Website.[63]

- As amazing (and tedious) as it may sound, US libraries don't use the ISBN! They use something called the **LCCN (Library of Congress Control Number)**. (In their defense, the LCCN has been around a lot longer than the ISBN; it's even undergone some modernization efforts in the last decade or so.)

> Would you recognize our government without its bureaucracy? The Library of Congress also uses a CIP number (Cataloging in Publication)[64] or a PCN (Preassigned Control Number)[65] for works that haven't been published yet. But as a self-publishing magnate, you shouldn't need these. There's also an ISSN[66] for serials!

Unfortunately, you can't apply for an LCCN as a self-publisher. But bear in mind that *you don't find eBooks on library shelves!* (Then they'd be books on CD or some such.) This only becomes an issue if you go the POD route. Then you can obtain an LCCN through one of the POD services (like Authorhouse or Xlibris).

- You can get an **SAN (Standard Address Number)** as well. This identifies you in the world of publishing by your address. Go through Bowker[67] to get it at a cost of about $150.00. But frankly, I've operated for quite a while without one. I wouldn't recommend it when you're just starting out.

- For tax purposes and in order to work with folks like Bowker and Lightning Source, you'll need to be an actual publishing house. But don't panic! This doesn't mean zillions of dollars; in Texas, it simply means that you need to go city hall and fill out an application for a DBA (Doing Business As). Starting *Forager Publications* cost less than $20. Call your local tax office to check the business requirements if you're not in Texas.

- You'll need a **website**. This can be simple, or it can be very complicated, but we'll cover the essentials.

We'll define a website as a "place" on the Internet accessed by a browser (Internet Explorer, Netscape, AOL, etc); it provides useful marketing and purchasing information about your book to a potential buyer. If you're reading this text in eBook format, you already know something about web browsing. (If you don't know anything about web browsing, you might want to reconsider creating an eBook; eBooks rely fairly heavily on the web.)

With some training, they're fairly easy to create and maintain. Bookstores and web stores (like Amazon.com) abound with how-to books for creating websites. For the most part, they're a waste of money. Here are the basic steps for creating a website:

1. **Create the page(s) you'd like.**

   Most people who've never done it panic when told they have to create a website. Creation involves a scary computer word – *programming!* But the web uses the most *simple* and forgiving of the programming languages – HTML (or Hyper Text Markup Language). For a set of simple tutorials on HTML, try the HTML Pit Stop.[68] Alternately, pick up a copy of *Sam's Teach Yourself HTML in 24 hours*.[69]

   > When faced with the option of a *Sam's Teach Yourself ... in 24 hours* (or *... in 21 Days*) book or something else, always opt for Sam's. Very few educational resources are better written. Another "always opt for" series is *Microsoft's ... Step by Step*. Then again, there're always those *One Step at a Time* books by that Sykes guy ...

If you intend your website as an advertising tool, you can ignore those other languages with scary letters like CGI, C++, XHTML and the like. You can accomplish any selling with links to Amazon or other websites that carry your material, or via PayPal, which provides the HTML code for you.

Countless programs flood the market to make your page design easier, but frankly, they're all improved with some knowledge of HTML.

Microsoft created one of the best (free) programs available for web page design in their **FrontPage Express**. Unfortunately, they soon realized that they could make money from the program and removed it from the market. It now sells (with some new bells and whistles) as **Front Page**. But if you can find the older Express (check Windows 98 install CDs and computers running Internet Explorer 4.0 or 5.0), you'll find quite an aide to your Internet advertising efforts.

2. **Find a web host.**

Once you've created your page, you'll need someone to *host* it for you. This means that you'll need someone to make your site available to Internet audiences. As with make-your-own-webpage programs, web hosts abound!

Look Closer!

Literally hundreds of website hosts blanket the web. When you look for one, you'll see the words *Free* and *Cheapest* on every one. Don't believe it. None are free and what you need will cost between $100 and $300 a year no matter whom you choose to host your site.

Things to look for when selecting a web host include:

- At least 1000Mb of web traffic per month. (I opted for 5000, and although I've come close a few times, I've rarely gone over the 1000 mark. Still, I have high hopes!) Web traffic is the amount of information transmitted over the host's lines. (Every time someone accesses your site, your pages transmit to their computer.)
- At least 100Mb of disk space on the host's server. Bare in mind that HTML pages are very small (or you're not doing them right) – usually less than 100kb (preferably less than 50kb). I opted for 100Mb and have gone over once or twice when I had to make large files available for customer/client downloads. But remember that I also put working files for my textbooks on my site for downloads; these are often several megabytes large.
- You may find an option for Resource Units as well. Unless you plan to use the site's tools for selling (or some other special activity), you won't have to worry about those.
- You must be able to use your own web name (called a *domain* or a *domain name*)! That is, potential buyers/readers/browsers must find you as www.[yoursitename].com. Don't use a site that requires the host's name first (as in www.aol.[yourname].com. These stand out as amateur sites and scream *cheap* to your potential customers.

For an additional charge (sometimes), many web hosts allow you to register your domain through them. This approach will save time and effort down the line. The charge is about the same everywhere, so you won't save any money going to one source to register the

name and another to host the site. We'll discuss more on name registry in Step 3.
- Your host should also provide email at your address. That is, you should be able to receive email at an address like sales@[mysite].com. I suggest getting an option that allows for ten email addresses (primary address, comments, sales, specials, book titles, webmaster, and anything else you might need).

I've used XO[70] as my host for several years now without complaint. Other host service companies include SBC Yahoo[71], Earthlink[72], Cheapdomain[73], Register.com[74], and of course, Microsoft[75].

3. **Register your domain name.**

   Select a domain name indicative of your work. I have used several that worked off of my primary XO account (foragerpub.com[76]). I still use UNeedCAD.com[77] (for my AutoCAD work), but I've eliminated most of the others as unnecessary expenses.

   Once you have an idea of what you'd like your domain name to be, go to one of the domain registry sites listed in the next paragraph and use their tools to be sure the name is available.

   As of this writing, Cheapdomain.com[78] charges $13.95 to register your domain name for a year, Register.com[79] charges $35/year. But before you register your name, see if your web host provides this service. (They often do it for free.)

4. **Upload your files.**

   Website hosts all provide some means of uploading your files (transferring your website files from your computer to their server where browsers can find them). I haven't found one whose uploading services were anything short of grossly inefficient. You can, however, download **FTP Explorer**[80]

(Figure 3.001), which makes uploading files as easy as using Windows Explorer to manage your computer files.

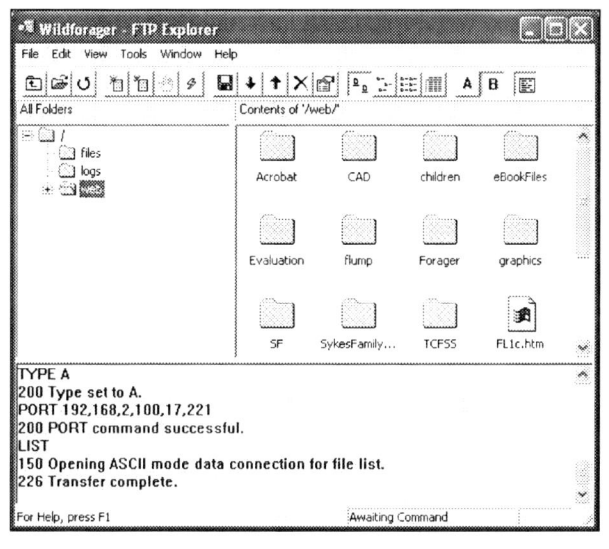

Figure 3.001

FTP Explorer is shareware with a 30 day trial period and $35 price tag after that. But the license is free for teachers, students, or school staff!

5. **List your site with search engines.**

   When you search for something using the Internet, your web browser (Internet Explorer, AOL, Netscape, etc.) sends your request to a *search engine*. These "engines" list millions of websites (together with their descriptions and key words) in massive databases. When your search matches one of the keywords connected to your site, it puts a *link* (what you pick on to move from one web page to another) to your site in the list of matches displayed by the web browser.

   Your web host will have tools to assist with listing your site with the major web engines (*Google*[81],

AltaVista[82], *AOL Netfind* [83], *Ask Jeeves*[84], *Looksmart*[85], *Netscape*[86], *Yahoo*[87], *WebCrawler*[88], etc.). Other places will offer to list your site with zillions of search engines ... at a price. Don't pay it. Just let your host take care of the work.

> Literally millions of new sites struggle to be listed with search engines every year. Virtually none are ever removed from the search engine's databases. Listing takes time – lots of time! If you think you may have a book ready this time next year, it's not a bad idea to register with the engines now. Then, you must be patient ... be *very* patient!

We'll discuss your website in more detail in Lesson 6.

That's a general run down of what you'll need to get started with marketing your book. (I wish someone had presented me with that list before I began ... then again, it might have scared me away from the whole idea!) The one thing I didn't discuss was fortitude! You have to be willing to work to market your books. Once you have all the tools in place (ISBN, DBA, Copyright, website, etc.), then you can actually start the real work – beating the streets for someone to buy your work.

That brings us to the final topic for this lesson – distributors and publishers.

Step 3.3 Publishers, Distributors, and Booksellers – A Brief Introduction

I've always had difficulty differentiating between publishers, distributors, and booksellers in my own mind, so let me start this section with some definitions.

- A **Publisher** prepares books, manuals, articles, etc. for distribution. (Printing lies in the publisher's realm of operations.)
- A **Distributor** markets what the publisher has prepared for distribution (in your case, your eBooks and PODs). That

is, the distributor is the middleman who takes the published material from the publisher and delivers it to the bookseller.
- A **Bookseller** sells your books (PODs or eBooks).

For years, the publisher has been a large house full of strangers who make anonymous decisions about your work. The distributor has always worked for the publisher or has been a shadow company under the publisher's umbrella. The bookseller has always been someone like Barnes & Nobles, BDalton, Waldenbooks, or that little corner bookstore you may remember as a kid (if you're as ripe as I am).

But now you're in the electronic age! You can publish yourself; indeed, you're reading this book because you want to be your own publisher. You'll also act to some extent as your own distributor and bookseller (but you'll keep considerably more of the profits than the big publisher allowed you). Still, help is available and, in some cases, necessary if you want to reach the lion's share of the market.

Let's take a look at some of the companies set up to help you.

- You've read bits and pieces about Lightning Source (LSI) throughout this book. What exactly is Lightning Source?

  Ingram (one of the major book distributors) began Lightning Source in 1997 as a *Print On Demand* operation. It still provides POD services to publishers, as well as being *the only source for eBooks used by Amazon.com*. (Read that last sentence again – it's of paramount importance to you as an eBook writer/publisher.) By our definitions, LSI (Lightning Source International) is both publisher and distributor.

  Lightning Source Pluses include:
  - Considerably lower pricing than other POD/eBook operations.
  - eBook services and pricing that beats everyone else by a landslide. The normal setup fee for eBooks is $25/title, but they've been running a special since I started with them several years ago, which allows them to waive the setup fee.

- Works with Amazon.com, Powells.com, and others to distribute and market your eBooks and POD books. They also work with Barnes & Nobles website[89] to sell your PODs. (Barnes & Nobles does *not*, however, sell eBooks.) I believe LSI and Amazon combine to make the largest distribution service of eBooks available in the world (but I haven't verified that information).
- Handles all the DRM (Digital Rights Management – aka. security) services for eBooks. You'll let them know what you want, and they'll do the rest for both Microsoft Reader and Adobe Reader formats.
- I've run into some hiccups working with the POD department at LSI (although they're getting better as we go), but the eBook department appears to be packed with professionals who know what they're doing and how to do it best!
- LSI books carry the publisher's label and/or logo. (They won't add an LSI logo unless you give them permission.) So the final purchaser can't tell that someone existed between them and the publisher.
- LSI automatically lists its eBooks and PODs at Amazon.com and Powells.com; it automatically lists its PODs at Barnes and Nobles and Borders books. PODs are also made available to bookstores via Ingram Books distribution services. (But don't let that fool you; they're clearly identified as POD books in the listings. We've already discussed bookstores' opinions of PODs.)
- Of course (as with most POD operations), you retain all rights for your work when you use LSI's resources.
- eBook royalties are negotiable. (I get a standard 45% on retail prices for all my eBooks. This percentage works well with Amazon requirements for sales.)

Lightning Source Minuses include:
- Lightning Source works with publishers. If you want to self-publish, you must be ... and behave like ... a publisher. This book details how to go about getting

yourself set up as a publisher, so you'll know what that involves. If you want to be an author with someone else doing the rest of the work, LSI isn't your best option.

- o   LSI doesn't publish color PODs, but has no problem with color eBooks.

> That being said, I have a news flash! LSI will begin handling full color texts soon (target is July of 2006). Color printing will be available for 8½ x 8½ or for 8½ x 11 paperback books only, but will allow full color throughout! (Now that's something to look forward to!)
>
> As of this printing, they have nothing available about pricing of color books, but you can contact them at: inquiry@lightningsource.com or call (615) 213-5815.

- o   LSI doesn't do layout work. It will not: layout your cover, layout your book, proofread or copyedit your book, or market your book. You'll be responsible for such things as selection of font types, margin setting, graphics location, spelling and grammar checking, and so forth. In short, you'll do the photographer's work, and they'll snap the picture. (You'll need to submit your POD work in one of the following formats: Adobe PDF, Adobe Postscript, or in the native formats from InDesign, Quark, or Pagemaker.)

I've worked quite closely with the people at LSI in the publication of several eBooks and PODs (my wild edible cookbook – *The Complete Forager, Spring/Summer Edition*, my science fiction novel – *The Vortex*, some eBook releases of my children's series – *F'Lump's Adventures with Timmy and Friends*, and of course my AutoCAD series). On the whole, and if you're willing to do your own setup work, Lightning Source will provide more bang-for-your-buck than any of the other publishers/distributors discussed here.

> Here's one of those little know tidbits that might help you decide on a publisher/distributor to help you –

> many of the POD houses use LSI resources to provide their services to their authors!

- For brevity's sake, I'll lump AuthorHouse[90], XLibris[91], iUniverse[92], Wheatmark[93], and the other POD organizations into one category. I've also worked fairly closely with AuthorHouse (in their original incarnation as 1stBooks), so I'll use them as my primary example. (Modest differences will exist between the various POD organizations, but I'll give you a general feel for what to expect. You can investigate each organization more thoroughly by visiting their website.)

As most POD organizations do, AuthorHouse works hard to cover all bases – publishing, distributing, and bookselling. This approach has many pluses with only one really serious minus – the cost.

Let's take a look. (AuthorHouse prices are current as of 4/30/06.)

AuthorHouse Pluses include:
  o AuthorHouse provides copyediting services to look for typos and errors. They'll charge a minimum of 1.5 cents per word (about $3.75 for a standard 250 word page). But bear in mind that if their copy editors, "determine the amount of editing needed is excessive"[*], their rates will go up. (Remember what I said about learning the tools of your trade!)
  o AuthorHouse will create your cover from scratch (although you are allowed to submit graphics toward that end).
  o AuthorHouse will fully format your book for you, and they allow submissions in word processor formats (Word or WordPerfect).
  o AuthorHouse provides the ISBN and bar codes as part of their standard package. They also provide an LCCN for an additional $75.

---

[*] AuthorHouse's Copy Editing Services Agreement (Rev Feb 22, 2005)

- AuthorHouse lists their PODs with Amazon.com, but not their eBooks. Find AuthorHouse (and other POD organizations) eBooks at eBooks.com[94]. (See more on eBooks.com below.)
- AuthorHouse will also copyright your manuscript for $150.
- AuthorHouse offers a host of marketing strategies ... at additional cost.
- AuthorHouse offers monthly specials to help with the financial end of their services.

AuthorHouse Minuses include:
- eBook creation comes at an extra $100 price tag, but must be accompanied by the $698 standard POD agreement.
- AuthorHouse doesn't produce color eBooks. Color PODs cost considerably more than the standard contract.
- AuthorHouse only pays 25% royalties on eBooks. POD royalties are negotiable.

I enjoyed my association with AuthorHouse (1stBooks). I published my first two novels with them (my children's books – *F'Lump's Adventures with Timmy and Tarbaby*, and *F'Lump's Adventures Continue with Timmy and Tarbaby*). I even purchased some advertising aides, but alas, to no avail. I lost hundreds of dollars in this first learning experience. (I made up most of it with the audio versions of these texts, which I later produced on my own.) My best advice concerning POD houses then is simply to watch the cost. You can do most of what they offer cheaper on your own ... if you're willing to do the work.

> Remember! After all the expenses involved with any setup – LSI or POD house – you still have to buy any printed books that you wish to sell on your own! (You'll receive royalties on books sold via Amazon or one of the other web-based booksellers, but LSI or the POD house will pay for producing the books sold

through these outlets.)

- One web-based bookseller outsells them all when it comes to eBooks (and apparently most other books as well) – Amazon.com[95]. Not only does Amazon serve as a primary bookseller, but you can watch your sales ranking fairly closely on your book's page. Amazon updates the rankings hourly, daily, or weekly depending upon the last rank available. You can also get a feel for how your book is received (and perceived) by the reviewer's comments and star rating on your book's page.

  LSI or your POD house will handle listing your book or eBook. But you'll have some work to do as well.

  o First, I recommend registering as a publisher with Amazon's Advantage[96] program. This enables you to offer books for sale yourself. (This is not a critical issue for eBooksellers; as I mentioned, LSI will take care of that part.) This will come in handy when you do the audio book version of your new book and offer it on CD. (I've made quite a bit more in the sales of audio books for my children's series than I have both through print or eBook format.)

  But of more immediate concern to you as a publisher is your access to the descriptions, publisher comments, cover graphics, and author comments sections of your book's Amazon page. These sections will prove critical in the sales of your eBook as you'll use them in much the same way you'd use the back cover of a printed book. Place your teasers, author credits, and cover information here.

  Amazon.com's Advantage program comes with a $29.95 price tag attached. They'll also take a 55% commission on your sales. On the bright side, this is the same 55% taken by LSI (or any other publisher) and is shared amongst those involved in the sales. You'll keep your 45% whether you work directly with

> Amazon or LSI. Additionally, any discounts offered at Amazon will come from their 55%.
>
> The $29.95 should be tax deductible as a marketing expense.

Once you've registered, sign in and select **Enhance Your Title's Detail Page**, then go to the **Book's Content Update Form**. You'll have to tell them which book's page you wish to edit, but then you can add/edit the information I mentioned in the last paragraph. When filling out your book's description, follow Hickory's advice: **Be Brilliant ... Be Brief**. You want to entice the buyer ... not bore them into looking at another book.

Be Brilliant!
Be Brief!

If LSI or your POD house hasn't provided a copy of the cover, you can upload it within the Advantage program. Be sure to follow the instructions closely as to size and format of the image or it won't get posted. Amazon requires the following in their cover graphics:

- 72 pixels/inch resolution
- Either a JPG or TIFF image
- The longest side should be 500+ pixels
- 8 channel, sRGB color mode
- Don't add borders to the graphic
- Use the ISBN as the file name

I've been quite pleased with the results of my collaboration with Amazon.com. I've made some money with them, and learned a lot about sales and marketing. I've also been able to use their feedback system to monitor how readers feel about my books, my publishing efforts, and eBooks in general. It hasn't all been good, but it has all been educational!

- Another tool that offers you an advantage is Amazon.com's Marketplace. Sign in as a normal user (book buyer) and go to **Your Seller Account**[97]. From here, you can sell your own books. (I've met one person who uses this approach exclusively and seems to do fairly well with it.) Amazon takes a generous chunk of the selling price, but they also provide a shipping allowance which works in your favor. I use the Marketplace to sell extra inventory or returned books – it works out to my advantage, as well!

- I won't spend much time on Powells.com, BarnesandNobles.com, or EBooks.com; unfortunately, none has anything like the Advantage program.

  Powells gets their eBooks and PODs from Lightning Source. They're fairly new to the market, but offer some much needed competition for folks like Amazon and Barnes & Noble. Before you buy at one of the other sites, check Powells for discounts!

  EBooks.com gets their eBooks from the POD houses (AuthorHouse and BookPublisher in the US, others overseas) as well as some of the high trade and academic publishing houses. Their lack of attention to the self- or small-publisher hurts both.

As it appears, your best bet as far as publishing and marketing help lies in the Lightning Source/Amazon.com combination. Although this arrangement doesn't suffer much from competition, their pricing is fair. (The 55% they take for their efforts is common in the Internet retail world of books – and still leaves you considerably more than the 5% to 12% you can hope to get from publishing houses.) Their work is professional and of good quality as well.

I've found the returns on my AutoCAD efforts to be only slightly less than I made with Prentice Hall (Pearson Education) as my publisher. I sell fewer books, but I keep considerably more per book (about 3x my Prentice Hall royalties), while my readers spend well under what Prentice Hall charged. (Readers can purchase the updated, 2007 material in eBook format for $38.90 for the two books. Prentice Hall's price for the 2002 version of the same material was $128.95 in two printed books. As I've indicated, I keep 45% – roughly $17.50 – when I sell both eBooks, while I receive between 5% and 12% of that same 45% – between $3 and $7 – in royalties when PH sells the printed version.)

Step 3.4 Summary

No one ever said self-publishing was cheap; and judging by the expenses chart that follows, this has been an expensive lesson! Well, bear in mind that you probably already have much of this material (your word processor, for example). Some of it you will absolutely need (again, your word processor) while some of it I recommend. Feel free to shop around for better prices (and let me know when you find them!). You may be able to pick up an older version of Acrobat from someone who's purchased a newer edition. And so many companies host websites these days that I'm almost sure you can find a better price than what I've listed here. (But remember to go with someone reputable.)

I've tried to list competitive prices throughout this lesson, but that doesn't mean that I've always found the best supplier. Use my list as a comparison when you shop around; if you find something better, good for you!

You won't face such a daunting ledger in our next lesson (although I will repeat some of what you've already learned about proofreading). There, we'll start the mechanics of putting your book together!

Visa, MasterCard, Bankruptcy Court …

Following is a list of expenses associated with Lesson 3. Bear in mind that these are only suggestions ... and that comparison shopping and careful deliberation about your specific needs might lower your expenses significantly!

Expenses Associated with this Lesson

Item	Min	Suggested	Max
Word Processor Application	0	109	299
Adobe Acrobat	9/mo	10/wk	449
Adobe Training (Text)	0	0	45
Clipart.com (images)	0	0	10/wk
Poser	0	250	250
Graphics Program	0	99	650
Proofreader	?	1/page	4/page
ISBN	0	25	225/10
Copyright	0	0	30
SAN	0	0	150
DBA	0	20	?
Website Host	0	300/yr	?
Domain Name	0	14/yr	35/yr
FTP Explorer	0	0	35
Totals (+/-)	**9**	**825+**	**2100+**

Lesson 4

Following this lesson, you will:

✓ Know how to format a book as an eBook or a POD

- o Fonts and Font sizes
- o TOC (page numbers, links, bookmarks, etc.)
- o Graphics and Illustrations (layouts)
- o Index
- o Links (other than the TOC)

✓ Know how a proofreader works

Preparing Your Text

Preparing your manuscript for publications requires two broad steps – **Preparing the Text** (grammar and usage), and **Preparing the Appearance** (setting the layout, fonts, table of contents, etc.). Each will take time, patience, and understanding on your part.

Your first impulse (especially if you're working with your first novel) will be to run, jump, and scream "Yea! I wrote a book!" But don't.

Oh, alright; go ahead. Be proud of yourself. Get it out of your system.

Now, take a deep breath and get back to work. You have a book to publish! (And it will no doubt change the world!)

Step 4.1 Preparing the Text

We've already spoken briefly about the importance of having your book proofread. You may know what you mean to say, but don't expect your reader to wade through grammatical gobbledygook to understand you.

A poorly written book will break your reader's heart!

Look at mastery of the language in a novel (or even in a technical manual) much as you might see love in a marriage. If it's there, it's only worth about 5% of the value (the rest is blood, sweat, and tears ... in marriage or manuscript); if it's absent, it's easily worth 95%, and the marriage (or manuscript) won't survive.

Of course you'll have to prepare your manuscript for the proofreader. I know, that sounds like having to clean up your room before the maid gets there. But proofreaders (and I suppose, maids) have their requirements. If they didn't, they might find themselves working with quarter-inch margins and single-spaced, 6-point fonts! (The poor maid might find herself facing my teenage son's bedroom!)

It's a good idea to ask your proofreader what he or she prefers in the way of document layout. But as a rule, you should double-space your manuscript on a standard 8½" x 11" sheet of paper.

Use 1" top/bottom and 1¼" side margins, number your pages (use any common placement for the page numbers), and use a 12-point font. Proofreaders prefer Times New Roman or Arial fonts. *If you want to get fancy with your layout, do it after you've had your manuscript proofread!*

Whether you hire someone to proof your manuscript or ask someone in your writer's group to help you, it's a good idea to know something about proofreader's marks. Here's a sample to help.

Mark	Means	Mark	Means
were/something	Separate	minute\ but	Delete
he	Capitalize	Normally / Normerly,	Fix Spelling
im[mediately	Close Up	that pirates lived	Italicize
ɟ inside.	Insert Period	here girl.	Insert Comma
"Pirates"	Make Bold	inside \Leaving	Paragraph
ɟackpack	Remove Cap	Sam(didn't)really)want	Transverse

Unfortunately, proofreaders' marks are not as universal as we might hope. You can find some other examples at these sites: Merriam-Webster Online[98], and The American Heritage® Dictionary of the English Language: Fourth Edition. 2000

(Bartleby.com)[99]. But once you've retained a proofreader or proofreading company, they should provide you with a copy of the marks they use.

In the last chapter, I also mentioned several ways proofreaders may charge you: by-the-page, by-the-hour, or by-the-word. Generally, by-the-page is the most common approach. You might save a little money by leaving the graphics out of the manuscript you provide.

Thanks, Hickory!

My AutoCAD texts ran upward of 2000 pages for all works. At $3/page, imagine what that would have done to my pocketbook! I still wouldn't be in the black. But without the several thousand graphics involved, it would be half that size and save me a bundle in by-the-page proofing costs. (Of course, I was lucky enough to be the offspring of a proofreading, red-headed tree frog who worked for my unending thanks ... and a few flies!)

Let your proofreader work unencumbered to do what you've hired him or her to do.

Here's a money making idea for hungry writers everywhere. Many (probably most) of you have liberal arts degrees. Post an ad at your local community college or university offering proofreading services for $1 or $1.50/page. You'll help some students with their grades and their financial wherewithal, make some money yourself, and (through competition) help bring the cost of professional proofreading down to an affordable level.

	Laying Out Your Manuscript for Publication
Step 4.2	**(Preparing the Appearance of Your eBook or POD)**

I always enjoy this part of my job. It means that, as a writer, I've finished a book. It's time for the publisher in me to go to work!

You'll wear a different hat now. The left-brained writer in you must sit silently by (for the most part), while the right-brained publisher dives into the nuts-and-bolts part of your job. (Talk about your mixed metaphors! I wonder if that one will make it past *my* proofreader!) This involves less creativity and more technical understanding of your tools.

Don't fret if you're not yet comfortable with your tools (Word Processors, Microsoft Reader, Adobe Acrobat, etc). It's a learn-as-you-go chore. (I've often repeated to my students that, when I go through a course without learning something new, I'll quit teaching it. The same holds true for most of my endeavors. Without learning new stuff, where's the fun?)

What you'll have to do now will depend upon several things:

- ◊ Will you prepare your manuscript for a Microsoft Reader or an Adobe Reader format?
- ◊ Are you preparing to turn your manuscript over to one of the POD houses or Lightning Source, or are you going to do it all yourself?
- ◊ Will you release a printed version of your eBook?

We'll consider each of these possibilities as we look at the nuts-and-bolts of preparing a manuscript for actual publication.

Let's get started.

- **Margins, Page Numbers, Headers, Footers, and Gutters**

    The good news: If you intend to create a Microsoft Reader file or to send your manuscript to one of the POD houses, you won't have to worry about these.

    Microsoft Reader reformats your manuscript with its own page numbers and margins. Gutters (those extra spaces you leave on the side of a page for binding) don't mean anything in an eBook format. Microsoft Reader ignores headers and footers, but it will pick up footnotes (although they don't necessarily fall at the bottom of the appropriate page).

The POD houses will format your manuscript for the binding size you request (or for an eBook). But check with them for their guidelines before you submit your work.

You'll need to set the margins, page numbers, etc. yourself if you intend to: use Adobe Reader, do it all yourself, or produce a printed version (POD) through Lightning Source.

You may think that using smaller margins will allow you to get more on a page (thus cutting down the ultimate cost of producing your book), but don't do it. Here's a tip from a pro: a few hundred extremely crowded pages intimidates a potential reader; *white space sells!* So add a few (or a few dozen) pages; you'll ease the strain on your readers' eyes and make them more inclined to buy your book.

I suggest 1¼" side margins (never less than 1") and 1" top and bottom margins. Place any headers no less than ¾" from the top of the page, and any footers no less than ½" from the bottom. These measurements should hold true for any size text – from 6" x 9" up to the 8½" x 11".

On the subject of headers and footers, don't go overboard. I placed a simple line at the bottom of the page in my SF novel; I thought it looked nice. But that silly line has been the subject of questions from every reviewer that has seen the book. I suppose it was needless clutter after all.

Limit headers, like book title or author's name, to every other page ... or don't use them at all. It's not like your reader doesn't know what he's reading. Some people like to put chapter titles in headings; this can be useful in a textbook, but otherwise will serve no real purpose. Limit this effort to every other page as well.

When writing a textbook, on the other hand, don't ignore the footnotes in favor of a non-cluttered page. This type of writing requires certain compromises. If you have "excessive" footnotes, consider making them endnotes instead (like the POD version of this book).

Center page numbers at the bottom of the page. It'll serve both as a locator for the reader and a subconscious target during reading.

- **Title Page**

    The title page of a print book serves no really useful purpose other than to repeat the cover on paper. In a POD, keep it simple. You can include a graphic if you feel that it's appropriate. Otherwise, just the title, author's byline, publisher's name, and copyright date are all you need. On an eBook title page, you can add some utility that a reader might appreciate.

    I sometimes use my Adobe Reader title page as something of a macro-TOC where I provide links to important sites within my eBook and strategically placed on my website.

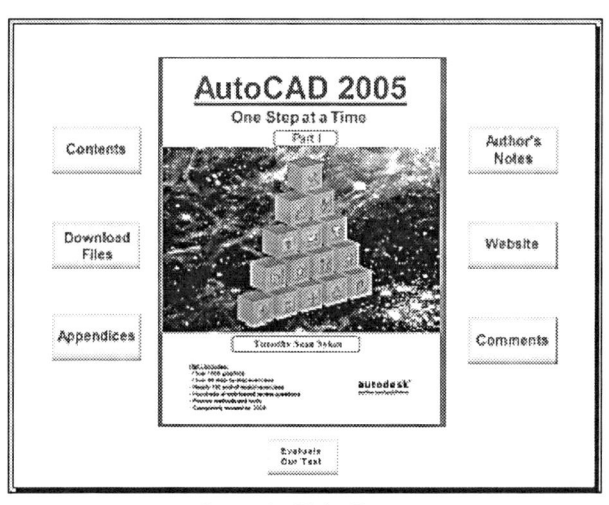

Sample Title Page

Consider the sample title page above. Here I provide a quick jump to the *Contents*, *Appendices*, and *Author's Notes* pages within the eBook. I also provide a link to *Download* [working] *Files* from my website, a link to visit my *Website* (where I can list changes or advertise a new release), and an email jump (*Comments*) that my readers can use to contact me. (I enjoy reader's comments and find them useful in keeping my text up to date.) As this is a textbook, I also provide access to a web-based evaluation form to help me learn what I've done right and what I need to do to keep my readers happy.

> Microsoft Reader reformats a document as it creates an eBook. Unfortunately, this means that you'll probably lose the layout on your title page; so don't go overboard in setting it up if you intend to use this format. Still, you can create a page with small linked graphics or simple text links to cover any needs like the ones I just discussed.
>
> I've seen this done both well and poorly. Should you opt for this approach, keep the text/graphics simple (short and sweet)! It looks better when centered on the page, as well.

We'll discuss hyperlinks in more detail in Links and Bookmarks below.

- **Table of Contents**

In a POD, the table of contents (TOC) should be complete and include section headings to the first or second level only. (More will increase you page count unnecessarily; fewer won't give the casual browser enough information to buy your book.) Include *accurate* page numbers (double check these thoroughly). You can decrease the size of the font (Times New Roman 11-point or even 10-point, but no lower) and use two columns if they'll fit easily to avoid adding too many pages.

If you've had the chance to read a couple of eBooks, you'll have discovered that a good table of contents is even more useful there than in a standard printed book. Both provide the same brief outline of the book's chapters, but when properly created, the eBook's TOC allows you to *jump* (via hyperlink) to the selected chapter.

You may have noticed that page numbers may vary (especially in the Microsoft Reader format) and text may reflow with different reader settings, so don't include page numbers in an eBook TOC. The reflow doesn't, however, affect the placement of hyperlinks and bookmarks, so readers really appreciate TOC links to help them locate a chapter.

How do you create a TOC with links? I suggest starting out with the word processor's TOC tools. Word automatically makes a table of contents complete with links, which (again, automatically) convert to links within your Microsoft Reader or Adobe Reader eBook. You can also use bookmarks (see Links and Bookmarks below).

You might want to consider adding just a bit more detail in your TOC than a print book might normally use. Remember that your reader can't thumb and quick-scan pages on his reading device. But don't go overboard; too much clutter hurts more than it helps. I like to include first and second level section headings, but I wouldn't go beyond that.

> Note: As I mentioned earlier, Microsoft Reader reformats a document in the process of creating an eBook. One of the things it does is to change the formatting usually associated with hyperlinks. (The blue color generally associated with links changes to an odd green, and the cursor doesn't change when passing over them.) The links still function, however, just as they would in any other type of document.

- **Font and Font Size, Boldface, Italics, Underlining, Color, and other Font Formatting Possibilities**

    I decided to use an unusual font (`Courier`) in the first POD book I published (POD format – *F'Lump's Adventures with Timmy and Tarbaby*). This led to some disparaging comments in a couple reviews. Courier, it seems, looks too much like it was created on an old fashioned typewriter.

    Two fonts seem to satisfy most readers (and reviewers) – Times New Roman (the most popular in printed texts and widely accepted in eBooks) and Arial (popular in print and eBooks). I've opted for Arial in most of my books primarily because I like the simple way it looks, but also because, when compared with the same size **Times New Roman** font, it appears larger. This makes it easier on my eyes.

Microsoft Reader converts all serif text to Berling Antigua (which resembles Times New Roman), san serif text to **Frutiger Linotype** (which resembles Arial), and monospace text to either `Courier New` (Pocket PC format) or `Lucida Sans Typewriter` (reader for PC).

By default, Microsoft Reader sizes text to get as close to 66 characters as possible on a line (33 characters on a Pocket PC). So you're sizing won't matter with this format. (Of course, the reader can resize the text as desired.)

For more on how Microsoft Reader formats an eBook, download the Microsoft Reader Layout Guide[100].

Adobe Acrobat, on the other hand, will use just about any font your word processor can use. But be aware that, just because it appears normal on your computer (where you created the word processor file) doesn't necessarily mean that it'll appear normal on someone else's screen.

Let me explain.

Unless told to *embed* fonts, Adobe Acrobat won't. This will reduce your file size (sometimes considerably), but it means that Adobe Reader will use the fonts on the computer containing the PDF to display the eBook. For this reason, you should stick with fonts that normally ship with a Windows system – such as Times New Roman or Arial.

I always embed font's for PDF files. POD houses and Lightning Source require it, and I'm assured that what I've created is what my reader will see.

I recommend sticking to a standard size font – usually ten-point to twelve-point. (I use a 14 point font in my emails ... but that's so that I don't have to grab my glasses to send notes.) Microsoft Reader users can resize the text as needed, but Adobe Reader users can't unless they're using the **Reflow** option. A ten-point Times New Roman font may save space, but it can be hard to see without zooming in awfully close ... even for the eagle-eyed among us! A twelve-point Arial appears quite large in comparison.

Don' t Be Cruel!

You're reading an eleven-point Arial in this text.

If you're considering providing a POD as well as an eBook to your readers, you'll need to think about how the type looks against the page as well. You'll also need to consider the number of pages. Most POD houses limit the size of a book to a maximum of 828 pages. Besides, they'll charge you by the number of pages in the book.

Both Arial and Times New Roman work well in print. But remember, a reader can't resize a ten-point Times New Roman on paper, and some of them will remember the eye strain next time they consider one of your books!

Both Microsoft Reader and Adobe Reader translate boldface, italics, underlining and color formatting fairly well. I have a problem with recognizing boldface on a Pocket PC, but that's probably due to my aging eyes rather than the software.

Although you probably won't use much in the way of text formatting in a piece of fiction, I will recommend standardizing your use of formatting techniques (especially in a textbook). (Use the *Styles* method when writing with the MS Word word processor.) Use formatting to lead your reader (that is, to make it easy for your reader to follow what you're doing), but don't clutter the page unnecessarily. In most cases, "Wow!" works as well as "***WOW!***"

- **Tables, Bullets, and Numbered Lists**

    Since works of fiction rarely use these tools, I'll concentrate on nonfiction works for this section.

    Tables, bullets, and numbered lists present no problem for a POD. When creating an eBook, however, you should consider several things.

    > One thing you should realize about these tools is that they don't show up well (okay, they look lousy) on a Pocket PC or any other handheld device. This holds true for both Microsoft Reader and Adobe Reader formats. Of the two, Adobe Reader handles them far better than Microsoft Reader.

    - **Tables**

        You won't find a better organizing tool in the world of textbooks. What's more, you'll find tables in virtually every field from Liberal Arts (English and History) to the Sciences. Unfortunately, they present a volume of problems for both creator and user when handheld devices come into play.

        The Pocket PC user must either pan the table across a 2" screen, or the reader simply refuses to resize the table at all making it impossible to read! Sometimes a single cell of the table tries to span several pages, while at other times the cell's contents might just disappear from the bottom of the page.

        For these reasons (and others), I strongly recommend the use of laptops or tablet PCs in the classroom!

        When targeting PCs, laptops, or tablet PCs, on the other hand, Adobe Reader handles tables quite nicely. (Microsoft Reader still has problems with cell content.) I make prodigious use of tables in all my AutoCAD texts (both print and electronic formats) and haven't faced a single glitch in the Adobe software because of them. In fact, tables were a primary reason for my selecting the Adobe format rather than the Microsoft Reader format.

Tables require no special set up procedure for PDF creation, although you might want to watch the extra spaces. (I like to place an extra space at the top of a cell if it lies directly below a header. This doesn't cause Adobe problems, but occasionally it will kick a row onto the next page.) If you intend to use Microsoft Reader, keep your row content short (three or four lines) and remember that Microsoft Reader attempts to limit a line to 66 characters (33 on a handheld device).

> Microsoft Reader 1.5 and subsequent releases support tables. Earlier releases did not. Don't assume your reader has the ability to perform this task on a handheld device.

- o **Bullets and Numbered Lists**

    Adobe Reader has no problem with bullets or numbered lists. In fact, as a rule where layout is concerned with Adobe Reader, you can assume that WYSIWYG holds true (pronounced *Whiz-ee-Wig* – or "What You See Is What You Get").

    Microsoft Reader, on the other hand, reformats bullets and numbered lists from your manuscript document. Primarily of concern to you is how Microsoft Reader handles indents associated with bullets and numbered lists; it eliminates them altogether.

    This doesn't have to be a major dilemma if you know about it ahead of time and know what to expect. I suggest limiting your use of bullets and numbered lists to primary sections. That is, avoid sub-bullets (as I've used in this text) or sub-numbers like those found in outline numbering.

    So with Microsoft Reader, you shouldn't use the addition or removal of indentations within the body of your manuscript to serve as section breaks.

- **Graphics and Illustrations**

    As I mentioned earlier where layout is concerned with Adobe Reader, you can assume that WYSIWYG holds true. This includes your layout of graphics and illustrations for both POD and eBooks.

The only real problem these additions might present in PDF format appears when viewing a PDF on a handheld device. Remember that the device, even in Reflow mode, can only do so much with the size of a graphic. Trying to view something created in 32-bit, high-resolution mode for a full-sized sheet of paper on a 2" x 3" 16-bit low-resolution screen doesn't always present pleasing (or even legible) results. So again, consider your target!

> When creating graphics, most people have a natural tendency to go with the best their computers can produce. Nowadays, this can mean resolutions approaching the infinite (and subsequent file sizes to match)!
>
> But consider these (Amazon.com's requirements for the cover image you'll submit to them):
>
> ◊ Resolution: 72 pixels/inch
> ◊ A length of 500+ pixels on the longest side (about 7" at 72 pixels/inch)
> ◊ RGB color mode
> ◊ 8 bits/channel
>
> These requirements produce a file size of less (often considerably) than 100k. (The same file created with a 300 pixels/inch resolution – over 32" on the longest side – is several megabytes large.) From this file, Amazon will create a thumbnail image – generally about 1k or 2k.
>
> Remember that graphics file size is the single greatest factor in the final size of your eBook! (Lightning Source limits the final size of your eBook to a maximum of about 8Mb.) I recommend shooting for a graphics file size of 20 to 30k whenever possible.

For Adobe Reader, create images that fit nicely on the page. (When preparing for a PDF format, I always place my graphics in a text box or a table to make them easier to handle.) If you hope to make your eBook translate well to a handheld device, center it on the page with text above and below (but not around) it. Make sure your images look good at both high and low resolution.

Microsoft Reader doesn't handle graphics nearly as well as Adobe Reader, and while the rules about resolution and file size apply, other rules are quite different.

When your target is Microsoft Reader, avoid placing graphics in text boxes or tables. Whenever possible, center or left-justify the graphic on a line by itself; that is, don't try to wrap text around it. Although you can wrap text with some difficulty, the results are often unpredictable.

Test and retest the final eBook to check the location of your graphics! Test the file on a PC, a laptop, and (if you wish to target it) a handheld device! Luckily, it's quite easy to produce the Microsoft Reader eBook, so this doesn't present a time or effort problem. But you might feel a bit put out if you have to recreate it a couple dozen times to get the graphics right.

When you're creating graphics for a POD, limit your resolution to 300dpi (dots per square inch) – lower if possible (150dpi works fine). You can also reduce file size by restricting yourself to black and white graphics. Some POD houses will allow color, but the price goes up dramatically. Unless you're producing a children's book, the color probably isn't necessary anyway.

- **Links & Bookmarks**

    Works of fiction probably won't make use of inter-document or even extra-document links beyond the TOC, so fiction writers (and of course, POD writers) can ignore this section. Additionally, bookmarks added by the reader in a Microsoft Reader eBook don't require any input at the time of creation.

    Links and predefined bookmarks in technical works, on the other hand, go a step beyond the TOC and the index in a printed book! You (the author) can provide your reader with *instant* access to anything you reference within the body of your eBook. This includes references to locations within your eBook (graphics, illustrations, chapter or section references, etc.) and references to sites on the Internet (reference articles, locations for further study of a specific topic, sales sites, invitations to visit your site or give you feedback, etc.).

Both Microsoft Reader and Adobe Reader handle links and predefined bookmarks so well that I had a hard time finding a down-side to using them; but there is one.

Links and predefined bookmarks take second place only to graphics when it comes to eBook size increasers. As much as I love using them ... and using them often! ... I occasionally find myself having to remove some of them to downsize my eBook file.

> Occasionally, I run into a problem creating a PDF with links in it. For some reason, Adobe places the actual link in some location other than atop the text. Let me explain.
>
> Adobe Acrobat creates an image of your page. After that, it will create a (generally invisible) link box – a boundary within which your reader will pick to go to the linked site. Ideally, this box should exist around the link text so that it appears that the reader actually picks on the text. Sometimes Adobe Acrobat hiccups and moves the link box toward the top of the page.
>
> The solution is simple enough – use Acrobat's tools to move the link box back over the text. Unfortunately, a new user without training or instruction (as I was when I began) doesn't know that.
>
> So if you create a PDF and discover that your linked text doesn't appear to work, don't panic. Follow this path within Acrobat (release 6):
>
> **Tools – Advance Editing – Link Tool**
>
> The link boxes will appear as rectangles on the page. Simply place your cursor over one and drag it to where it belongs.

- **Indices**

    Again, works of fiction generally don't use indices, so here's another section you fiction writers can ignore.

    The electronic format of an eBook makes searching for specific information (via the Search procedures we discussed in Lesson 2) even easier than using an end-of-text index. An index in an eBook, then, would be an unnecessary redundancy. Further, it would require increasing your page count and file size unnecessarily. So unless you intend to create a POD along with your eBook, you can forgo this chore!

    If, on the other hand, you intend to create a POD version of your textbook or technical work, you might want to include an index. Luckily, you have a couple options that might save you some time and money.

    ◊ First, use the Indexing tool that comes with your word processor (in MS Word, use the **Insert** pull down menu and select **Reference** ... **Index and Tables**). This eases the pain of index creation somewhat, although you'll still have to spend some time with it. (You can hire someone to create an index for you, but this is all they'll do – except for lowering your bank balance.)

    ◊ If you attach the index to the end of your POD, you'll have to pay for a few extra pages of printing. You can do this – and your readers will appreciate it – or you can save a few dollars by listing a web address at the end of the POD inviting your readers to download the index from your website.

Step 4.3	Summary

Once you've read this lesson, you should be able to get your manuscript ready to convert to an eBook or a POD. I'd recommend skimming the next lesson (*Converting Your Text*) before you prepare your manuscript, however, as it may give you some insights into where you're going with your efforts. Then come back to this lesson and follow it carefully.

I suggest you *not* jump in and start formatting text and moving graphics and creating tables all at once. Take one thing at a time – complete your text formatting before looking at tables; then complete your tables before dealing with graphics placement, and so forth.

Above all – never *work with the only copy of your manuscript!* For sanity's sake, keep a pristine copy of your book somewhere safe. I strongly recommend you keep both a printed and an electronic copy in a secure location (free from possible virus infection or meteor strike).

Expenses Associated with this Lesson

Item	Expense (USD)		
	Min	Suggested	Max
Proofreader	?	$1/page	$4/page

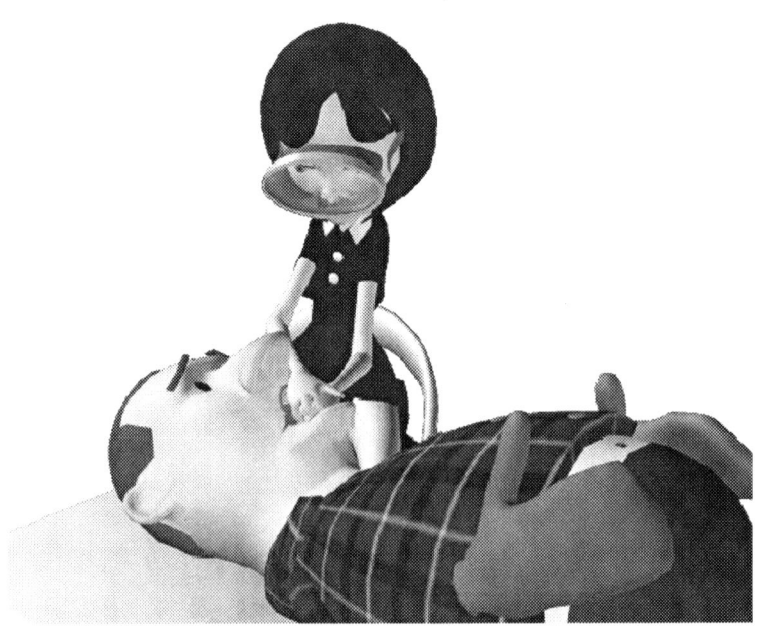

Work - It's Like Pulling Teeth!

Lesson 5

Following this lesson, you will:

- ✓ Know how to convert your manuscript to a Microsoft Reader format

- ✓ Know how to convert your manuscript to an Adobe Reader format or POD setup

Converting Your Text

After all the effort you've made to prepare your manuscript for conversion to an eBook, the actual conversion may seem anticlimactic. In the case of Microsoft Reader, it requires pushing a button. Adobe has a few additional requirements, but depending upon your target, can be just as easy.

To make it easier to understand, we'll look at the conversion procedures for each reader separately.

Step 5.1 Converting to a Microsoft Reader Format

Microsoft provides three guides to assist in creation and conversion of manuscripts to Microsoft Reader (.lit) files. This section summarizes these guides, but you can download them in their entirety from these locations: Microsoft Reader Layout Guide[101] (120 pages – MS Word format or .lit), Microsoft Reader Source Materials and Conversions Guide[102] (50 pages – MS Word format or .lit), and Microsoft Reader Markup Guide[103] (177 pages – MS Word format or .lit).

To create a Microsoft Reader formatted eBook, first create your manuscript in MS Word 2002 or 2003. (You might be able to find someone who will convert a Quark XPress, HTML, Pagemaker, or Framemaker file, but they'll charge you for doing it. Microsoft provides a list of third party content conversion providers[104] at their website.) Then complete the preparations for conversion detailed in Lesson 4.

Download

Read Button

You'll use a free add-in (*Read In Microsoft Reader* – or *RMR*) to create your eBook. Download the RMR from this site: http://www.microsoft.com/reader/developers/downloads/rmr.asp. Once downloaded, double-click on the *WordRMR.exe* file to install the add-in. This places a **Read** button on the MS Word Standard toolbar. You'll use this button to do your conversion.

Use the RMR when you wish to create a work of fiction in a popular, easy to use format – the Microsoft Reader *.lit* file. As you discovered in Lesson 2, Microsoft Reader provides a user-friendly interface for PC, laptops, or handheld devices. The low learning curve and availability of many diverse works of fiction using this format ensure that your book will be in good company (and that the format won't disappear from the marketplace in the foreseeable future).

Download	You can, if you wish, use your own MS Word document for the following exercise. If so, you'll need the following graphics (as jpg, gif, or png files): • Cover – measuring 510 x 680 pixels • Thumbnail – measuring 99 x 132 pixels • Cover Standard – measuring 82 x 680 pixels (required only for Microsoft Reader 1.5) Alternately, you can use our files. Download these from our website (http://www.foragerpub.com/eBookFiles): *Pirates.doc, pirates_cover.jpg, pirates_cover_standard.jpg,* and *pirates_thumb.jpg.* I suggest putting them in a separate, easily accessed training folder.

(Now we can get to the easy part.)

Do This: 5.1.1	**Converting a MS Word File to a Microsoft Reader (.lit) File**

I. If you haven't already done so, download and install the RMR.[105]
II. Open the document you wish to convert in MS Word. I'll use the *Pirates.doc* file.
III. Follow these steps.

TOOLS	STEPS
Read Button	1. Pick the **Read** button on the Standard toolbar. Read In opens a Read In Microsoft Reader dialog box (below). We'll take a few minutes to look at this dialog box and get it ready to create our eBook.

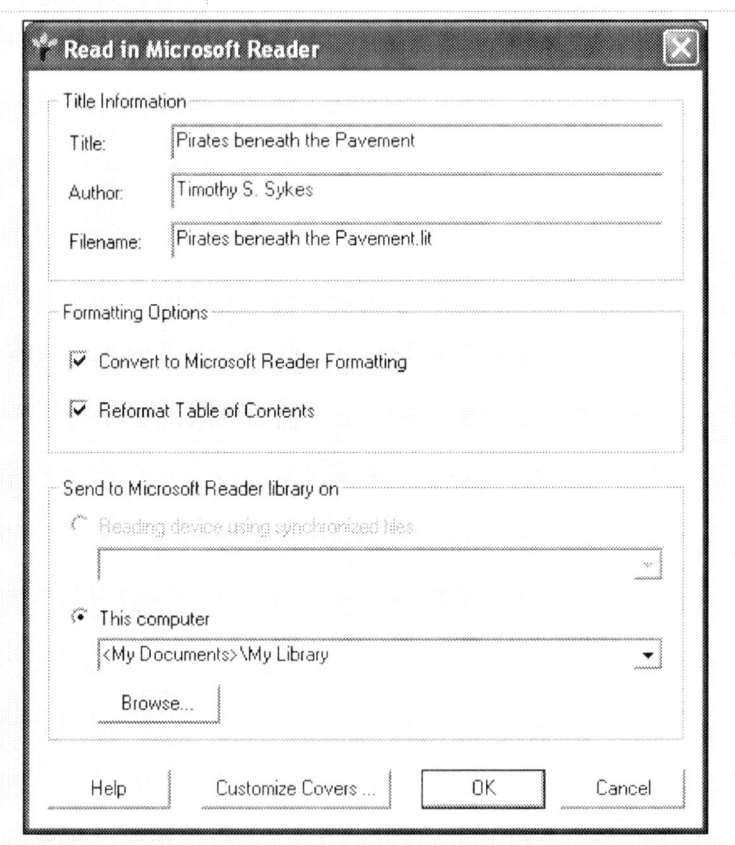

Read in Microsoft Reader

Title Information
- Title: Pirates beneath the Pavement
- Author: Timothy S. Sykes
- Filename: Pirates beneath the Pavement.lit

Formatting Options
- ☑ Convert to Microsoft Reader Formatting
- ☑ Reformat Table of Contents

Send to Microsoft Reader library on
- ○ Reading device using synchronized files
- ⦿ This computer
  - <My Documents>\My Library
  - Browse...

Help | Customize Covers... | OK | Cancel

2. If the **Title Information** frame hasn't been filled in with the appropriate information, fill it in now. (Read In will mine the document's properties for the information and automatically fill in the **Title Information** frame with available

TOOLS	STEPS
	data. It will create a file name from the document title, and place the .lit extension on it.)
	3. You have two **Formatting Options**: - **Convert to Microsoft Reader Formatting** – A check in this box tells Read In to remove all styles that conflict with Microsoft Reader defaults (ie. the hidden formatting for font-family and line-height). Read In will also translate specific font sizes into relative sizes so that your reader can adjust the view to his own preferences. Removing this check will result in a larger eBook file size and can potentially cause Microsoft Reader problems. I wouldn't recommend it unless you're absolutely sure of your target and your reader's preferences. - **Reformat Table of Contents** – A check in this box allows Read In to translate your TOC into something it can use. Without this conversion, the links between TOC and chapters might not function. (As the *Pirates* story has no TOC, this tool will have no effect on it.) We'll leave both options checked.
	4. The next frame – **Send to Microsoft Reader library on** – allows you to specify where Read In will place the .lit file. With a bullet next to the first option – **Reading device using synchronized file** – you can send the new eBook directly to your

113

TOOLS	STEPS
	handheld device. The second option – **This computer** – directs the file to a folder which you can select with the **Browse** button. We'll accept the default folder location.
[Customize Covers ...]	5. Finally, you'll find four buttons across the bottom of the Read In dialog box: • **Help** presents a Windows standard Help screen with information about the Read In tool you're using. • **Customize Covers** takes you to a dialog box where you'll specify the cover(s) for your eBook. • **OK** completes the process and begins creation of your eBook. • **Cancel**, of course, interrupts the process and returns you to MS Word. Let's proceed by picking the **Customize Covers** button; we'll set up our eBook cover now. Read In presents the Cover Graphics dialog box (next figure).

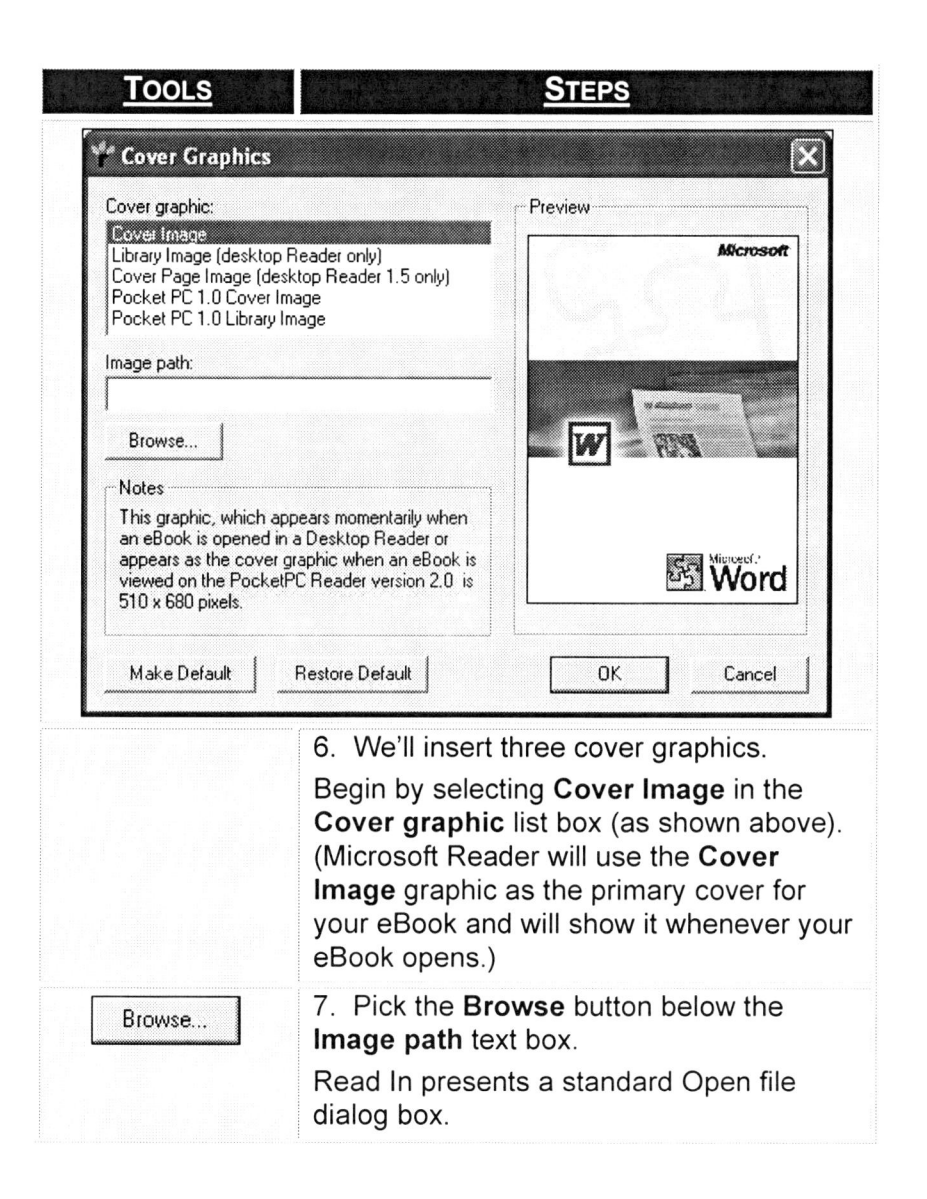

TOOLS	STEPS
![Cover Graphics dialog box showing Cover graphic list with "Cover Image" selected, Image path field with Browse button, Notes section reading "This graphic, which appears momentarily when an eBook is opened in a Desktop Reader or appears as the cover graphic when an eBook is viewed on the PocketPC Reader version 2.0 is 510 x 680 pixels.", Preview pane showing Microsoft Word cover, and Make Default, Restore Default, OK, Cancel buttons]	6. We'll insert three cover graphics. Begin by selecting **Cover Image** in the **Cover graphic** list box (as shown above). (Microsoft Reader will use the **Cover Image** graphic as the primary cover for your eBook and will show it whenever your eBook opens.)
Browse...	7. Pick the **Browse** button below the **Image path** text box. Read In presents a standard Open file dialog box.

115

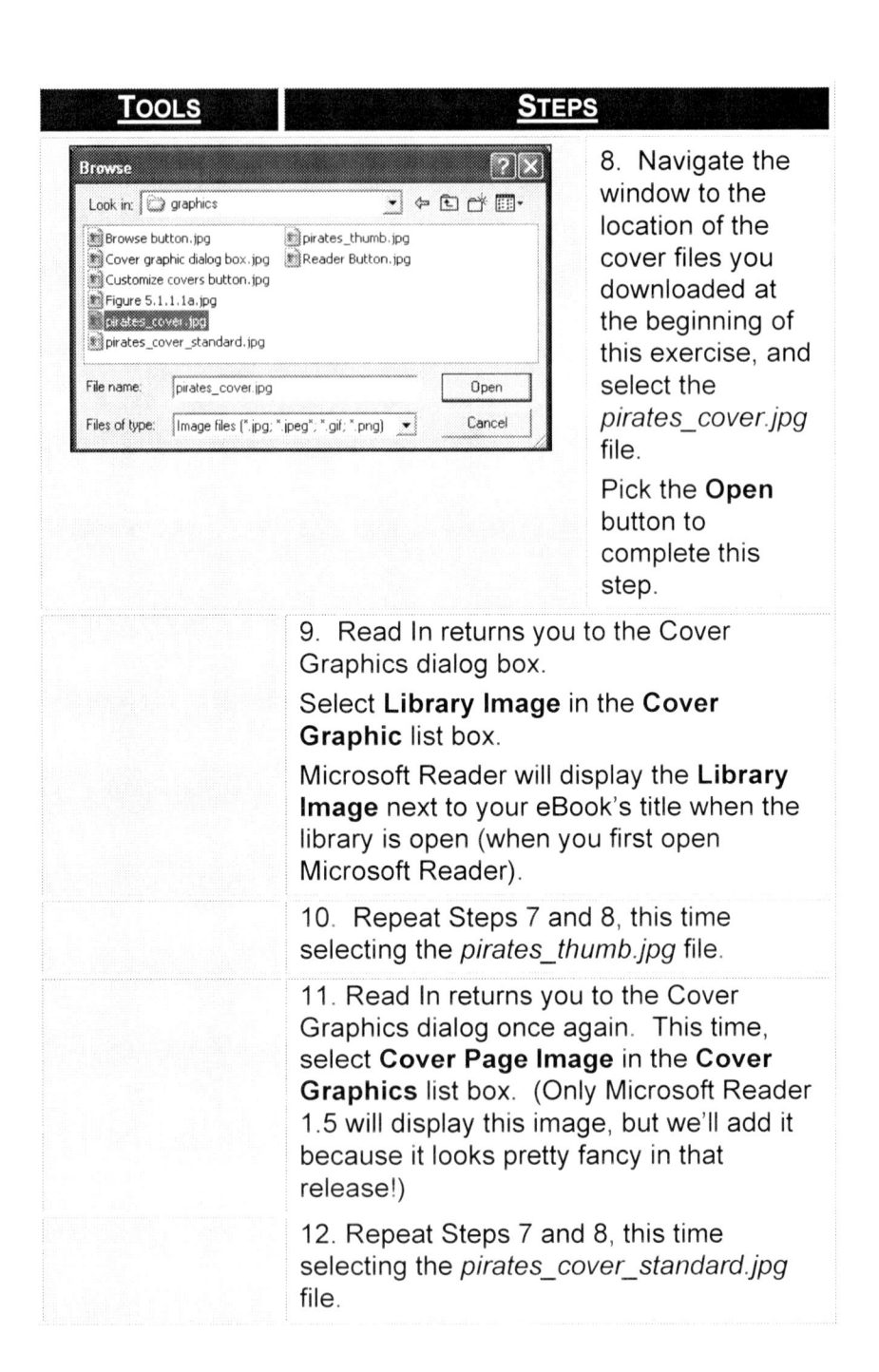

TOOLS	STEPS
![Browse dialog box showing graphics folder with pirates_cover.jpg selected]	8. Navigate the window to the location of the cover files you downloaded at the beginning of this exercise, and select the *pirates_cover.jpg* file. Pick the **Open** button to complete this step.
	9. Read In returns you to the Cover Graphics dialog box. Select **Library Image** in the **Cover Graphic** list box. Microsoft Reader will display the **Library Image** next to your eBook's title when the library is open (when you first open Microsoft Reader).
	10. Repeat Steps 7 and 8, this time selecting the *pirates_thumb.jpg* file.
	11. Read In returns you to the Cover Graphics dialog once again. This time, select **Cover Page Image** in the **Cover Graphics** list box. (Only Microsoft Reader 1.5 will display this image, but we'll add it because it looks pretty fancy in that release!)
	12. Repeat Steps 7 and 8, this time selecting the *pirates_cover_standard.jpg* file.

116

TOOLS	STEPS
	13. Read In returns you to the Cover Graphics dialog box. If we wished, we could add a cover graphic and a thumbnail graphic specifically for a handheld device, but without them, Microsoft Reader will simply resize the graphics we've already added. Pick the **OK** button to return to the Read In Microsoft Reader dialog box.
OK	
OK	14. That's it! Pick the **OK** button once again, and Read In will create your eBook! When it has finished, Read In will display the dialog box shown below. Pick the **OK** button in this dialog box; Microsoft Reader now opens and you can begin reading your new eBook! (If you have several eBooks on your system, look for the new one at the end of the list.)

Read in Microsoft Reader

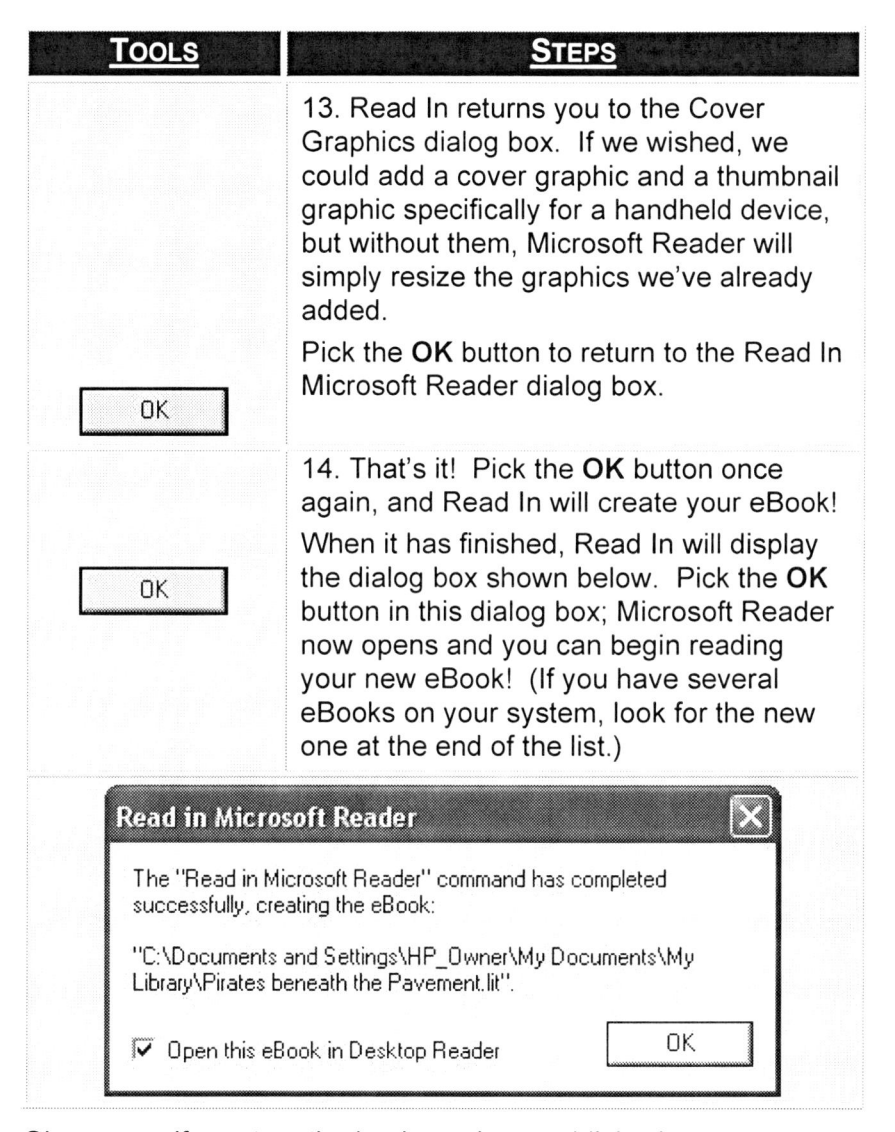

The "Read in Microsoft Reader" command has completed successfully, creating the eBook:

"C:\Documents and Settings\HP_Owner\My Documents\My Library\Pirates beneath the Pavement.lit".

☑ Open this eBook in Desktop Reader   OK

Give yourself a pat on the back; you're a publisher!

Step 5.2 Converting to an Adobe or Acrobat Reader Format

You'll probably find the Adobe Acrobat approach fairly complicated at first. But if you're creating a textbook or manual with tables, a great number of graphics or illustrations, bullets, or numbered lists, or if you're creating a POD for Lightning Source to produce, you'll have to take some time to acclimatize yourself to this remarkable tool.

We'll go through two tutorials. First, I'll show you the inexpensive approach using the Create Adobe PDF Online tool[106]. Then we'll discuss the pluses and minuses of this approach. In the second tutorial, I'll show you how to create your PDF eBook using Adobe Professional (the expensive approach). Adobe Standard procedures are about the same as Adobe Professional's, so those of you who opted for the recommended purchase back in Lesson 2 won't be without instruction!

Step 5.2.1	Converting to a PDF Using the Adobe PDF Online Tool (Adobe eBooks or Print Files for PODs)

Adobe's PDF Online Tool provides almost everything you'll find in the Standard or Professional versions (at least in the creation category), but it has a couple *critical* limitations.

You cannot create a PDF of more than 100 pages (with the paid subscription – 50 pages with the trial). Children's books probably won't present a problem, nor will essays or most theses. That major novel, however, will require more of an investment (or less if you opt for the Microsoft Reader approach). Textbooks will also require at least the Standard Edition.

Another limitation appears if you try to choose the free approach and use the demo to create a quick eBook. The demo doesn't add tags. Tags are tools required to reflow text and use hyperlinks within a PDF document; without them, you're reader won't be able to use a handheld device or use those inter- (or extra-) document links.

An even more critical limitation with the web-based tool lies in your inability to edit a document after creating it. Without that ability, you'll find yourself recreating the PDF for every fix you make – much as you'll do with Microsoft Reader.

Let's convert our *Pirates.doc* story to a PDF format using Adobe's PDF Online Tool. (Note: I've used the Free Trial for this demo; you may have some additional options with the subscription.)

| Do This: 5.2.1.1 | Converting a MS Word File to a PDF Using Adobe's Online Tool |

I. Open your browser and go to the Adobe website (http://www.adobe.com).
II. Follow these steps.

TOOLS	STEPS
Create Adobe PDF Online	1. Look for the **Create Adobe PDF Online** access button (webpage-creators love to change things around, but as of this writing, it's in the lower left quadrant of the page). Pick it.
	2. Your browser now displays a Sign In page. Sign in if you already have an Adobe User ID and password, otherwise, select the **get an Adobe log in** link (below the password text box) and provide the required information to get your User ID/password. Then return here and enter them in the appropriate boxes.
	3. Your browser now displays the Initial Screen (see the following figure). Let's set your **Preferences** first. (Select the **Preferences** link on the right side of the page.)

Convert a File
Select a file from your hard drive, and we'll create an Adobe® PDF file for you. We can also do optical character recognition (OCR) on image files.

Convert a Web Page
Enter the URL of a Web page, and we'll capture it as an Adobe PDF file. You can then save, distribute, or print it.

Conversion Choices
Conversion Status
Conversion History
Preferences

Subscribe and Get More!
Become a Create Adobe PDF Online subscriber and get additional features and benefits.

Use Create Adobe PDF Online as a desktop printer
Use Create Adobe PDF Online to convert your documents to Adobe PDF files from your desktop.

119

TOOLS	STEPS
(screenshot of Preferences page showing Current Account Limits, Create Adobe PDF Online Printer Settings, Document Options, Paper Capture Options, Password Security Options, and Service Options)	4. The Preferences page presents some information about the limits of your account and several options for your conversion. Pay close attention to these.

- At the top of the page, you'll find your **Current Account Limits**. Shown here are the standard limits for the free trial.
- **Document Options** include **Web**, **eBook**, **Screen**, **Print**, and **Press** settings. Each option includes several default settings (font embedding, image compression, color handling, etc.). Adobe has optimized each option with the best settings for that effort. You can change them, but without some training, you'll probably be better off accepting the defaults for **eBooks**.
- **Paper Capture Options** include such things as paper size and OCR (Optical Character Recognition) settings. Accept the default.
- We'll look at **Security Options** in more detail in Step 6.
- **Service Options** include delivery method (how will Adobe deliver your PDF file to you) and how long will it

TOOLS	STEPS
	be available at the Adobe site. Accept the defaults except for: • Change the Optimization settings to eBook • Change the **Delivery Method** to **Email me my new PDF as an attachment**. This means that you won't have to return to the website to download the resulting file. (Note: Our *Pirates.pdf* will be a small file. If your document produces a larger file – over 1Mb, your ISP may not accept the email.)

Before continuing to the security settings, understand that your distributor (Lightning Source or one of the POD houses) will expect a file free of security. It makes life easier on them if you allow them to set up the security options they'll provide for you. This works in your favor in two ways – less work for you in setting up security options, and the final security (set up by LSI or your POD house) will be of a much higher quality than yours could be.

If, however, you intend to distribute your eBook on your own, study one of the Adobe Acrobat textbooks to learn how to get the most out of these settings.

	5. Let's take a better look at those **Security Options**. Pick the **No Printing (128-bit)** security option and then the **edit settings** link just beside that (refer to the image in Step 5). (The **128-bit** option provides more security than the **40-bit** option but requires Adobe Reader 5.0 or later. But since the Adobe Reader doesn't cost your buyer anything, it's safe to opt for the higher settings.) Your browser presents the Advanced Settings page (below).

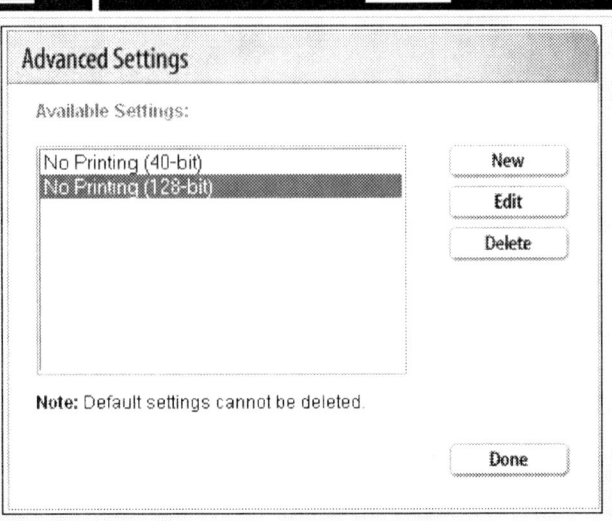

TOOLS	STEPS
![Advanced Settings dialog showing Available Settings with "No Printing (40-bit)" and "No Printing (128-bit)" highlighted, with New, Edit, Delete, and Done buttons. Note: Default settings cannot be deleted.]	
	6. Be sure the **No Printing (128-bit)** option is highlighted, and then pick the **Edit** button.
	7. Your browser presents an Edit Settings screen (see the following figure).
	• Here you can set your file so that a potential reader needs a password to **Open the Document**. I don't recommend using this option. If readers are going to pass your eBook around, they can as easily include the password. Legitimate readers, on the other hand, might find the password a nuisance.
	• You can also set your file so that readers can't change your security options without a password. If you need to include security in your document, you'll need to insure that the bad guys can't easily change it. Enter the required password in the **Specify Password to Change the**

TOOLS	STEPS
	Security Options text boxes.
- You can change the level of security encryption here making it more difficult to break. But remember that higher levels of security require more recent versions of the Adobe Reader. 128-bit is the highest currently available.
- You should leave the **Content Access for the Visually Impaired** enabled. It doesn't really hurt your security and it might help someone read your book who might not otherwise be able.
- **Allow Content Copying and Extraction** is the key to your security. If enabled, you can individually control printing. Your options include **Not Allowed**, **Low Resolution** only, or **Fully Allowed**. You can also control exactly what changes can be made to your document. These options include:
- **General Editing, Comment and Form Field Authoring** (essentially full editing features)
- **None**
- **Only Document Assembly**
- **Only Form Fill-in or Signing** (good if you've included a feedback form with your eBook)
- **Comment Authoring, Form Fill-In or Signing** (this allows the reader to add comments to your eBook as he reads – providing he is reading with Adobe Acrobat Standard or Professional).

TOOLS	STEPS
	I'll remove the check and not **Allow Content Copying and Extraction**. I don't have forms in my *Pirates* eBook, and I don't want readers to print it.

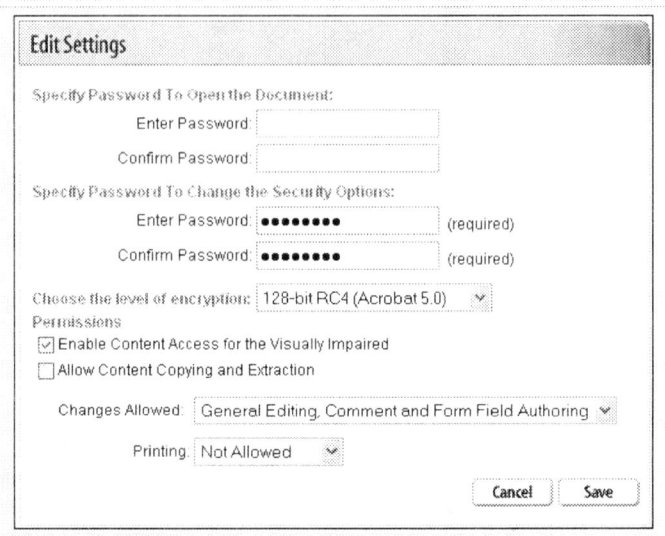

[Edit Settings dialog screenshot]

8. Pick the **Save** button to save your security settings. Adobe asks for a settings name (below). Give it something you can identify later, and pick the **OK** button to continue.

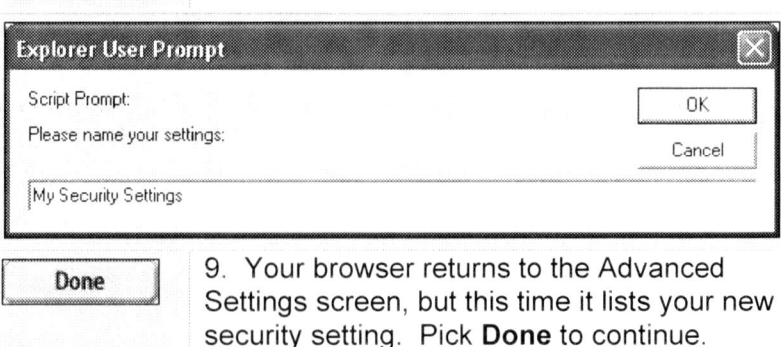

[Explorer User Prompt dialog screenshot — "Please name your settings: My Security Settings"]

Done	9. Your browser returns to the Advanced Settings screen, but this time it lists your new security setting. Pick **Done** to continue.
OK	10. Your browser returns to the Preferences screen. Pick **OK** to continue.

124

TOOLS	STEPS
Convert a File Select a file from your hard drive, and we'll create an Adobe® PDF file for you. We can also do optical character recognition (OCR) on image files.	11. You've set up your preferences, and your browser now returns to the initial screen. Now we can begin to create our eBook. Pick **Convert a File**.
Submit	12. Adobe presents a Terms of Use agreement. Read it over, place a check next to *I Accept the Adobe Online Services Additional Terms*. Then pick the **Submit** button.
	13. Repeat Step 11.
	14. Your browser presents a Select a File screen (see the following figure). Pick the **Browse** button.

Select a File

Click Browse to select a file to convert.

[   ] [Browse...]

Supported File Types

[Cancel] [Continue]

Open	14. Windows presents a standard Choose File dialog box. Navigate to the folder where you've placed the *Pirates.doc* file. Select it and pick **Open**.
Continue	15. Your browser returns to the Select a file screen. Now the **... file to convert** text box shows your file (*Pirates.doc*). Pick **Continue**. (You may face a bit of a delay at this point while the file uploads to the website.)

TOOLS	STEPS
	16. Your browser now presents a Conversion Settings screen (see the following figure). You can make any final adjustments here before continuing. When you're ready, pick **Create PDF!**

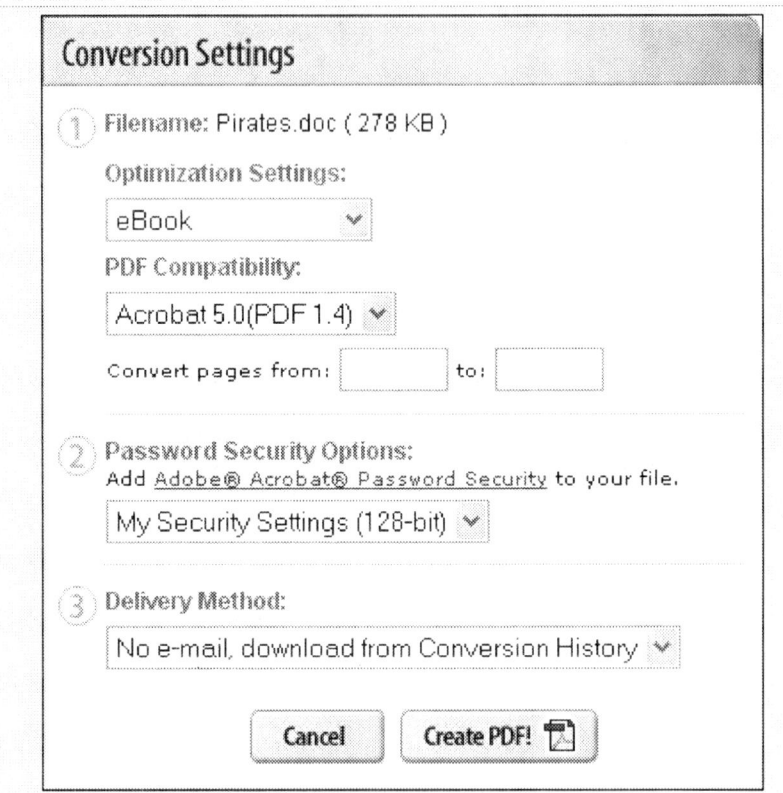

> **Conversion Settings**
>
> ① Filename: Pirates.doc (278 KB)
>
> Optimization Settings:
> [eBook]
>
> PDF Compatibility:
> [Acrobat 5.0(PDF 1.4)]
>
> Convert pages from: [   ] to: [   ]
>
> ② Password Security Options:
> Add Adobe® Acrobat® Password Security to your file.
> [My Security Settings (128-bit)]
>
> ③ Delivery Method:
> [No e-mail, download from Conversion History]
>
> [Cancel]   [Create PDF!]

| | 17. Finally, your browser presents a Confirmation screen (see the following figure). Here you'll receive a **Document ID**, which you can use for tracking if you have any problems, as well as delivery information for your PDF. |
| | Close the window when you've finished and watch your email! It takes about five minutes or so for the *Pirates.pdf* file to arrive. When it |

Tools	Steps
	does, open it in your reader and look it over. Try to copy part of the text. Can you do it? (I hope not! We set it up to prevent copying!)

Confirmation

Conversion Details:

           Document ID: 445119D7-2197-28423F
       Delivery Method: Conversion History
Conversion Will Start In: now

Note: Converted Adobe PDF files must be picked up within 72 hours.

You'll find that the PDF you've created has some very wide margins. I set it up to print as a 6" x 9" POD (if I care to go that route). I can trim the margins back for my eBook if I have access to the Adobe Acrobat Standard or Professional edition (but if I had access to one of those, I'd have used it rather than the online tool).

Remember that Adobe doesn't reformat your document for you as Microsoft Read In does, and you cannot edit a PDF using the Adobe Online Tool. The solution – *make sure you're document is properly (and fully) set up before you create the PDF (your eBook)*.

On the plus side – you can create a fully operational PDF (with or without security) for sale, distribution, or to pass on to Lightning Source or a POD house, and the $9.95/month price tag won't place your pocketbook in an iron lung!

Let's take a look at the same procedure using Adobe Acrobat Professional.

Step 5.2.2	**Converting to a PDF Using Adobe Acrobat Professional (or Standard), Release 6 or 7**

Okay, so you've splurged and bought the big biscuit – Adobe Acrobat Professional 6 (or 7). (I admire your confidence!) I'll walk

127

you through the same basic procedure we used with the Online Tool, but I still recommend a course or one of the how-to manuals to get all of the intricacies of this marvelous tool. Try the *Adobe Acrobat 6.0* [or *7*] *Classroom in a Book* for either the Standard or Professional editions (about $45 before discounts), or *How to Do Everything with Adobe Acrobat 6* [or *7*] (about $25).

If you wish to create a PDF from an MS Word (2000 or later) document, you can open the document within Word and use one of the Adobe PDF buttons placed there when you installed Adobe Acrobat Professional 6.0 (or 7.0).

First, however, you should set up the PDF using the **Change Conversion Settings** option found under the Adobe PDF pull down menu (also added when you installed the Acrobat software). This will present a dialog box to help you with your setup. The dialog box options resemble those you used with the Online Tool. (Unfortunately, the first thing you may notice is that eBook isn't one of your setup options. But we'll look at how to deal with this in our exercise.) You'll find this method fast and easy.

> This exercise will work as well for the Standard edition, although the interfaces may appear slightly different. Unfortunately, it will *not* work for earlier releases of Adobe Acrobat because releases 6 and 7 have some major interface differences (they look different from earlier releases).
>
> Users of an earlier release of Adobe Acrobat should pick up an appropriate manual for that release (the two titles mentioned previously also exist for Adobe Acrobat 5.0).

Do This: 5.2.2.1	**Creating a Setup for Converting Your Document to a PDF Using Adobe Acrobat Professional 6 or 7**

We'll begin by setting our preferences for PDF creation, and then we'll convert our *Pirates.doc* file to an eBook.

I'll detail three different approaches to setting security and opening the Adobe PDF Settings dialog box –

   a) from within MS Word (Steps 1a)

   b) from within the PDF print option found in most applications – including WordPerfect (Steps 1b)

   c) from within Adobe Acrobat Professional (Steps 1c)

Of course, only one approach is necessary to create your eBook, but this method saves repeating several steps later. To accomplish your goal, simply select the approach you'd like to use and select the appropriate first steps – 1a, 1b, or 1c.

Then I'll explain how to adjust your settings for an eBook (Step 2 and beyond).

I've taken the screen captures in section from Adobe Acrobat Professional 7.07, but the differences between these and their 6.0 counterparts, where they exist at all, are minimal. I'll point out any major changes as I go.

    i.   Follow these steps to create your conversion settings from within MS Word 2003. *(The MS Word 2002 procedure will be similar.)*

STEPS

1a – 1. From the **Adobe PDF** pull down menu in MS Word, select **Change Conversion Settings**. Adobe opens the Acrobat PDF Maker (see the following figure).

STEPS

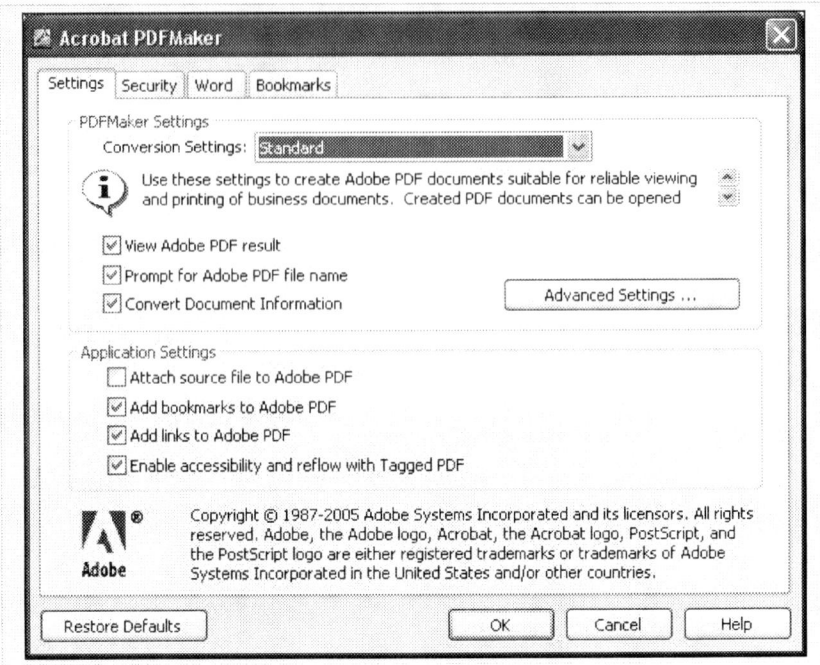

1a – 2. In the **PDF Maker Settings** frame of the **Settings** tab, select **Standard** in the **Conversion Settings** selection box. (Acrobat doesn't provide the **eBook** option you saw in the Online Tool, which is based on the 5.5 release.) We'll come back to the **Settings** tab in a minute.

1a – 3. Pick the **Security** tab (see the following figure). If you intend to pass your eBook along to Lightning Source or one of the POD houses, leave this tab free of passwords. Otherwise, feel free to secure your eBook as you consider necessary.

STEPS

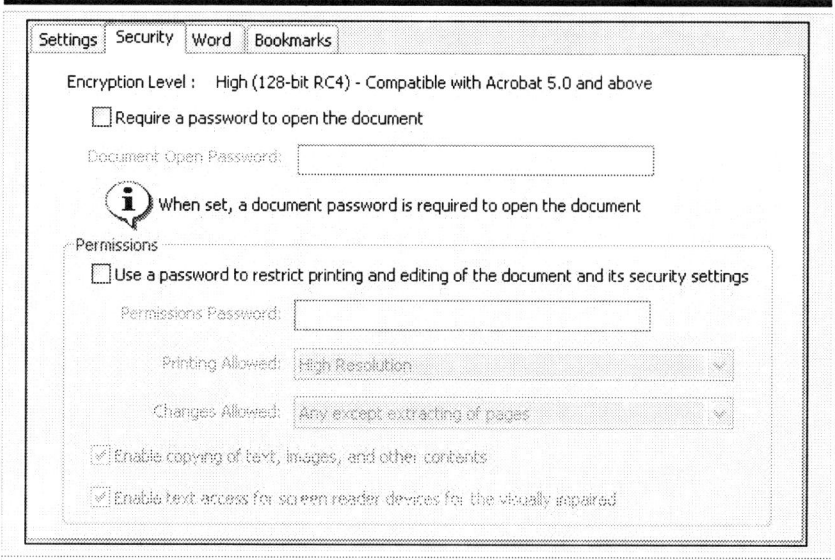

![Security tab dialog showing Encryption Level, password options, and permissions settings with tabs for Settings, Security, Word, and Bookmarks]

1a – 4. Pick the **Word** tab (see the following figure). These are your options:

- **Convert displayed comments to notes in the PDF**: An eBook generally doesn't have comments in the manuscript that you'll need to convert to PDF notes, so you can remove this check.

- **Convert linked text boxes to article threads**: (This option is not available in Release 7.) I haven't found a reason to link text boxes in a manuscript, so I remove this check as well. (Article threads work something like "automatic" columns in a newspaper – when you reach the bottom of one column, Adobe Reader will automatically take you to the top of the continuation column.)

- **Convert cross-references and table of contents to links**: Leave this box checked so that your readers can pick on a TOC or cross-reference link to go to the referenced page.

- **Convert footnote and endnote links:** links footnotes and endnotes to the appropriate citation in the text. (I

STEPS

usually leave this checked out of habit; although I rarely use footnotes or endnotes, I have used them in my textbooks and been frustrated when they didn't convert.)

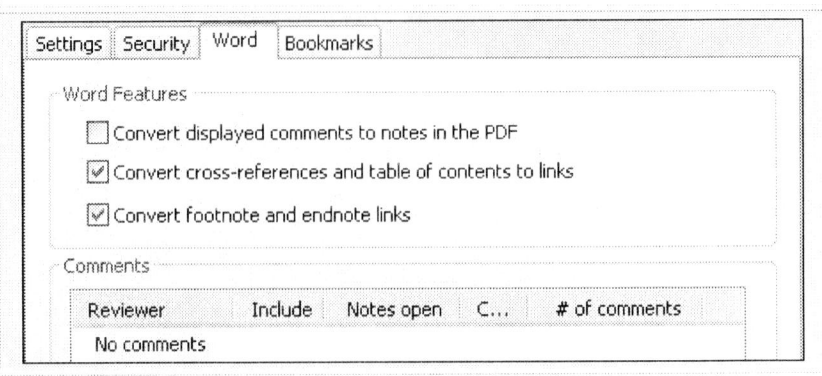

| Settings | Security | Word | Bookmarks |

Word Features
- ☐ Convert displayed comments to notes in the PDF
- ☑ Convert cross-references and table of contents to links
- ☑ Convert footnote and endnote links

Comments

Reviewer	Include	Notes open	C...	# of comments
No comments				

1a – 5. Pick the **Bookmarks** tab (see the following figure).

Most people use headings to indicate the beginnings of chapters or sections. As these are good starting or stopping places in a book, they are appropriate places to bookmark. I leave the check next to **Convert Word Headings to Bookmarks** for my eBooks, although I seldom leave Xs in any but the **Heading 1** or **Heading 2** boxes.

I use far too many Word Styles (text styles in MS Word) to want to bookmark them. Too many bookmarks may require your reader to bookmark the bookmark page! Clear the check box next to **Convert Word Styles to Bookmarks**.

| Settings | Security | Word | Bookmarks |

Bookmark Options
- ☑ Convert Word Headings to Bookmarks
- ☐ Convert Word Styles to Bookmarks

Element	Type	Bookmark	Level
Heading 1	Heading	☒	1
Heading 2	Heading	☒	2
Heading 3	Heading	☒	3

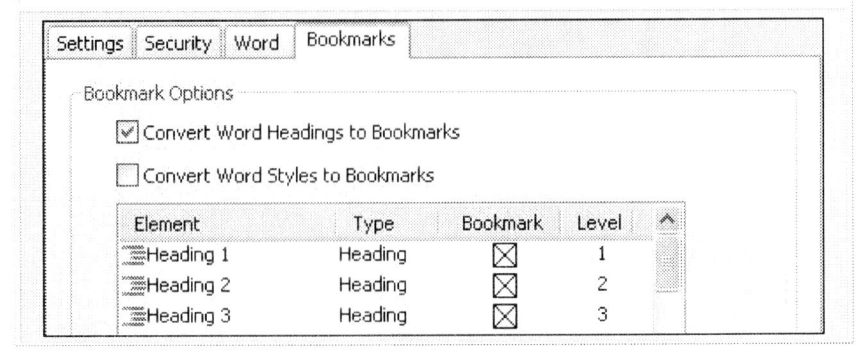

STEPS

1a – 6. Return to the **Settings** tab (see the following figure). You'll make some key decisions on this tab, and you'll go from here to the Adobe PDF Settings dialog box.

First, consider your options in the **PDFMaker Settings** frame.

- Leave your **Conversion Settings** selection on **Standard**. Acrobat 6.0 doesn't have an **eBook** option, so we'll have to set things up ourselves.
- A check next to **View Adobe PDF result** causes Adobe to open and display your eBook once the conversion has been completed.
- You can remove the check next to **Prompt for Adobe PDF file name** if you wish. Without it, the filename will default to the Word document filename with a PDF extension. (I prefer to be prompted.)
- **Convert Document Information** simply means that Adobe will record such things as the Author data from the Word document. You can alter this information later using tools within Adobe Acrobat.

Now we'll consider your options in the **Application Settings** frame.

- Don't **Attach source file to Adobe PDF**. This unnecessarily increases the size of the file while providing no benefit to you or your reader. (This is occasionally a helpful tool in business.)
- If you've added links and/or bookmarks inside your eBook, you'll want to include checks next to the last three options – **Add links to Adobe PDF**, **Add bookmarks to Adobe PDF**, and **Enable accessibility and reflow with Tagged PDF**.

STEPS

```
Settings | Security | Word | Bookmarks
  PDFMaker Settings
    Conversion Settings: Standard
      (i) Use these settings to create Adobe PDF documents suitable for reliable viewing
          and printing of business documents. Created PDF documents can be opened
      [✓] View Adobe PDF result
      [✓] Prompt for Adobe PDF file name
      [✓] Convert Document Information          [ Advanced Settings ... ]
  Application Settings
      [ ] Attach source file to Adobe PDF
      [✓] Add bookmarks to Adobe PDF
      [✓] Add links to Adobe PDF
      [✓] Enable accessibility and reflow with Tagged PDF
```

1a – 7. Pick the **Advanced Settings** button to continue to the Adobe PDF Settings dialog box, and then proceed to Step 2.

    ii.   Follow these steps to create your conversion settings from within the **Adobe PDF Printer** option of most applications.

This step will accomplish the same thing you did in Steps 1a, but here you'll approach PDF creation from the **Printer** option of any application supported by Adobe Acrobat; I'll use MS Word 2003, but the steps are the same for most applications.

STEPS

1b – 1. Select **Print** from the File pull down menu. Your application will display the Print dialog box.

1b – 2. In the **Printer** or **Destination** frame of the **Main** tab (depending on your application), select the down arrow next to the **Name** selection box. From the popup list, select **Adobe PDF** as shown in the following figure.

STEPS

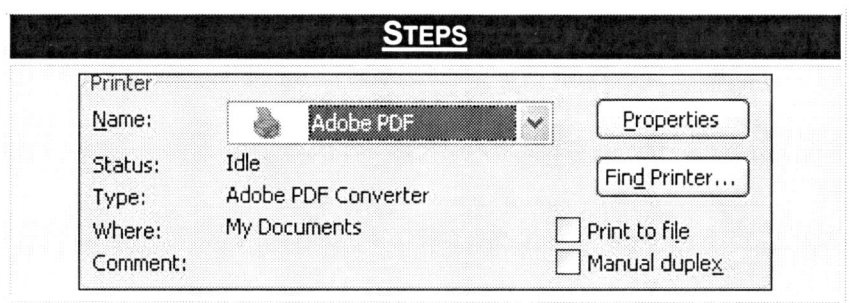

```
Printer
Name:        [Adobe PDF      v]      [ Properties  ]
Status:   Idle
Type:     Adobe PDF Converter        [ Find Printer... ]
Where:    My Documents               [ ] Print to file
Comment:                             [ ] Manual duplex
```

1b – 3. Pick the **Properties** button next to the **Name** selection box to open the Adobe PDF Document Properties dialog box (see the following figure). Notice the tabs; let's take a look at each.

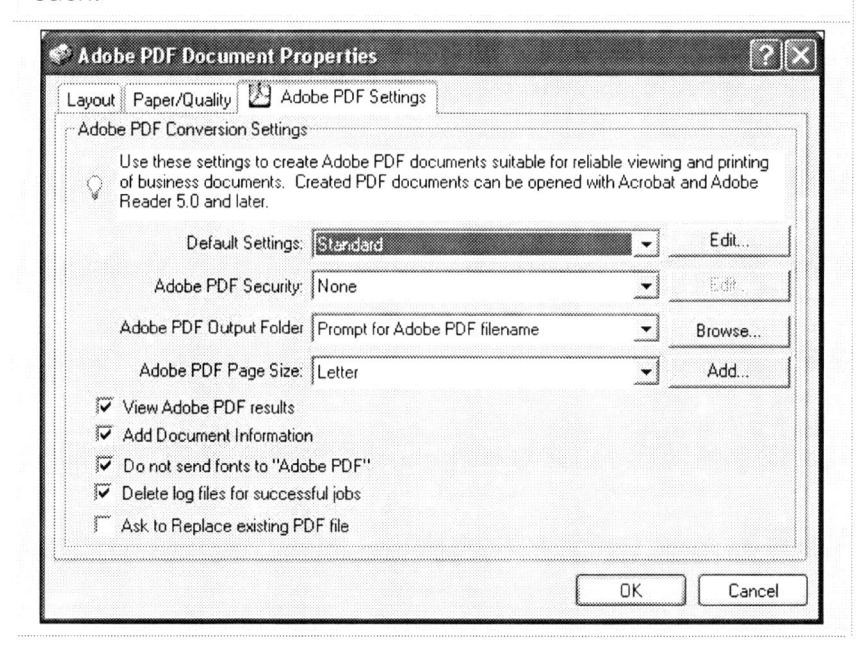

Adobe PDF Document Properties

Layout | **Paper/Quality** | **Adobe PDF Settings**

Adobe PDF Conversion Settings

Use these settings to create Adobe PDF documents suitable for reliable viewing and printing of business documents. Created PDF documents can be opened with Acrobat and Adobe Reader 5.0 and later.

Default Settings: [Standard]   [Edit...]
Adobe PDF Security: [None]   [Edit...]
Adobe PDF Output Folder: [Prompt for Adobe PDF filename] [Browse...]
Adobe PDF Page Size: [Letter]   [Add...]

[✓] View Adobe PDF results
[✓] Add Document Information
[✓] Do not send fonts to "Adobe PDF"
[✓] Delete log files for successful jobs
[ ] Ask to Replace existing PDF file

[OK] [Cancel]

135

STEPS

1b – 4. On the **Layout** tab (see the following figure), select the layout **Orientation** for your eBook. We'll use **Portrait** for our *Pirates...* eBook.

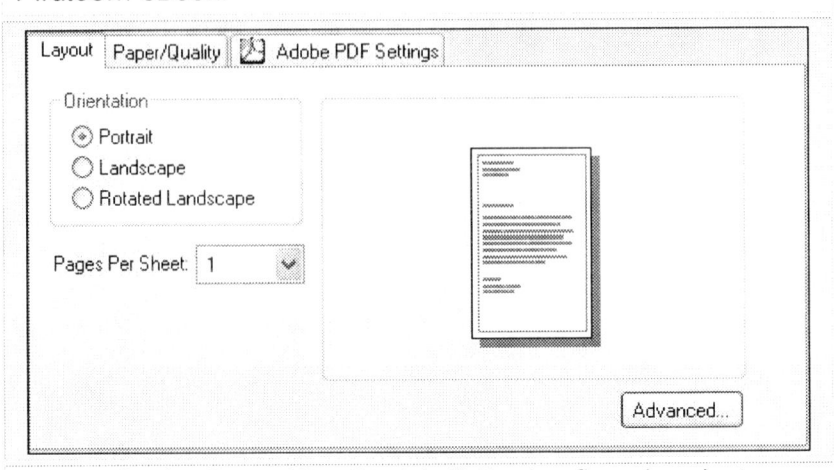

1b – 5. On the **Paper/Quality** tab (following figure), select whether your eBook will be color or black and white. Color results in a considerably larger file size but looks nicer. I usually opt for the color setting unless I'm preparing a POD (most POD houses require black and white or charge you heavily for color). I can always use grayscale graphics if the need arises to reduce my file size.

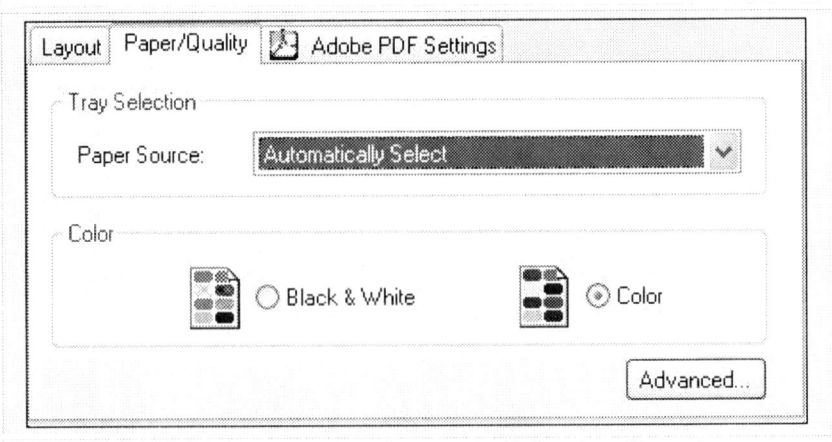

1b – 6. The **Adobe PDF Settings** tab (following figure)

STEPS

contains most of the meat-and-potatoes of the Adobe PDF Document Properties dialog box.

- Select the **Adobe PDF Page Size** from the control box. I always opt for the default (**Letter**) size and make adjustments (crop the size) as an edit once I've created the PDF. (I've run into margin problems adding a **Custom Page** at this point.)

  (Note: Lightning Source requires that eBook pages be the default 8½" x 11", with equal margins, and contain no cropping or crop marks.)

- The bottom three options contain one, which is critical, and two that are less important.
  - I suggest sending fonts to the PDF (remove the check next to **Do not send fonts to "Adobe PDF"**) – this insures that your eBook's appearance will be consistent on different computers.
  - I generally **Delete log files** ... as I rarely need to reference them.
  - If you remove the check next to **Ask to Replace existing PDF file**, you'll overwrite any files that you've already created by the default name. This saves effort later (to delete older files), but it also makes comparison with a previous setup more difficult.

- The **Adobe PDF Settings** tab contains several control boxes you'll use to select the **Standard Default Settings** ... and then edit them. It also contains a control box for adjusting the **Adobe PDF Security** settings in your eBook. (This procedure is identical to that covered in Step 1a-3.) Finally, you'll find a control box for setting the **Adobe PDF Output Folder**. Here, you'll tell Adobe to **Prompt** [you] **for a filename** or to use the document's current filename (with a PDF extension) and put the file in the My Documents folder.

  Below the control boxes, you'll find the final two check

STEPS

boxes for this procedure.
- **View Adobe PDF Results:** if checked, Adobe will display your new eBook as soon as it has created it.
- **Add Document Information** works like the **Convert Document Information** option did in Step 1a-6.

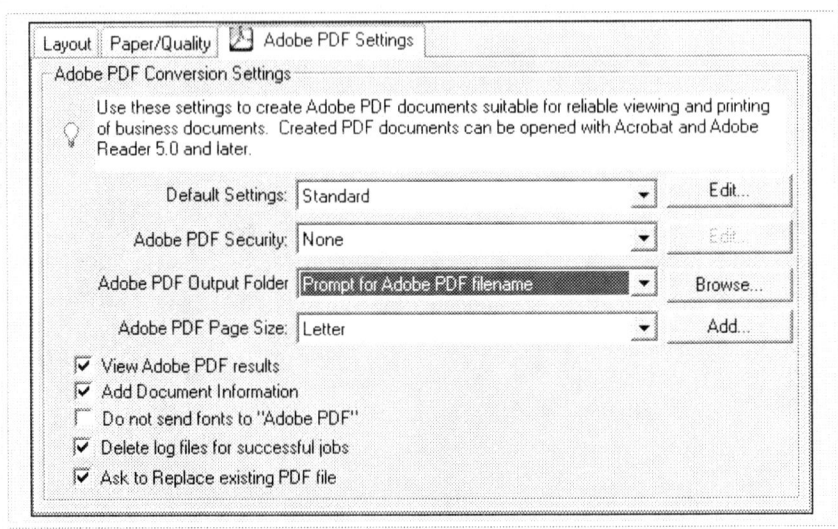

```
Layout | Paper/Quality | Adobe PDF Settings
─ Adobe PDF Conversion Settings ─
    Use these settings to create Adobe PDF documents suitable for reliable viewing and printing
    of business documents. Created PDF documents can be opened with Acrobat and Adobe
    Reader 5.0 and later.

        Default Settings:  Standard                         ▼   Edit...
        Adobe PDF Security: None                            ▼   Edit...
        Adobe PDF Output Folder: Prompt for Adobe PDF filename ▼ Browse...
        Adobe PDF Page Size: Letter                         ▼   Add...

    ☑ View Adobe PDF results
    ☑ Add Document Information
    ☐ Do not send fonts to "Adobe PDF"
    ☑ Delete log files for successful jobs
    ☑ Ask to Replace existing PDF file
```

1b – 7. Select the **Standard Default Settings**, and then pick the **Edit** button next to it to proceed to the Adobe PDF Settings dialog box. Proceed to Step 2.

iii. Follow these steps to create your conversion settings from within Adobe PDF Professional 6.0. This step will accomplish the same things you did in Steps 1a and 1b, but here you'll approach PDF creation from within the Adobe Acrobat application. From there, you can import a file from any Adobe Acrobat supported application.

STEPS

1c – 1. From within Adobe Acrobat, select the **Preferences** option from the Edit pull down menu.

1c – 2. Adobe presents the Preferences dialog box. Notice

STEPS

the many options available in the left-most column (another argument for taking a course or picking up a training manual specifically for Adobe Acrobat). Select the **Convert to PDF** option in the left column, and then select the **Microsoft Office** option in the center column (as shown).

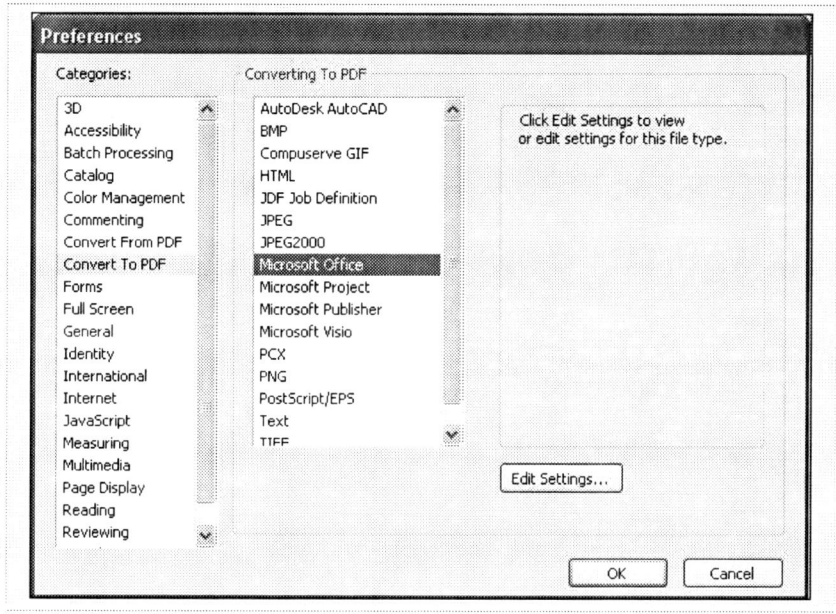

1c – 3. Pick the **Edit Settings** button to continue. Acrobat presents the Adobe PDF Settings for supported documents dialog box (following figure).

- As we did in Steps 1a and 1b, we'll use the **Adobe PDF Settings** selection box to begin with a **Standard** setup.
- You can use the **Adobe PDF Security** control box to set up security for your eBook. Using the **Edit** button next to this option, you can call the same **Security** tab/dialog box that similar buttons or links called from the MS Word and Print procedures.
- The check next to **Enable accessibility & reflow** enables the reflow option we saw in Lesson 2.
- Leave the check next to **Add bookmarks and links to**

STEPS
Adobe PDF file if you've used bookmarks or links in your document that you wish converted in your eBook. • You won't need to add a check next to the **Convert entire Excel spreadsheet** for an eBook. (Even if you're writing about Excel spreadsheets, you'll import them into your word processor before creating your eBook.)
Adobe PDF Settings for supported documents dialog box showing: Adobe PDF Settings: Standard; Adobe PDF Security: None; checked: Enable accessibility and reflow; checked: Add bookmarks and links to Adobe PDF file; unchecked: Convert entire Excel workbook; OK / Cancel buttons.
1c – 4. Select the **Standard** option in the **Adobe PDF Settings** selection box, and then pick the **Edit** button next to it to continue to the Adobe PDF Settings dialog box. Proceed to Step 2.

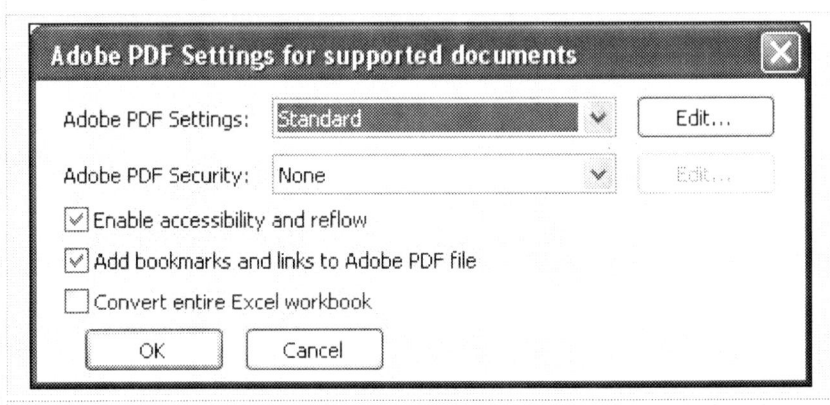

iv.   Okay, let's complete the conversion setup!

TOOLS	STEPS
	2. Regardless of the path you took to get here, you've finally arrived at the Adobe PDF Settings dialog box. (Phew! What an effort!) Let's start with the **General** folder. (This is a tab in Acrobat Pro 6, but the options will be similar). See the following figure.

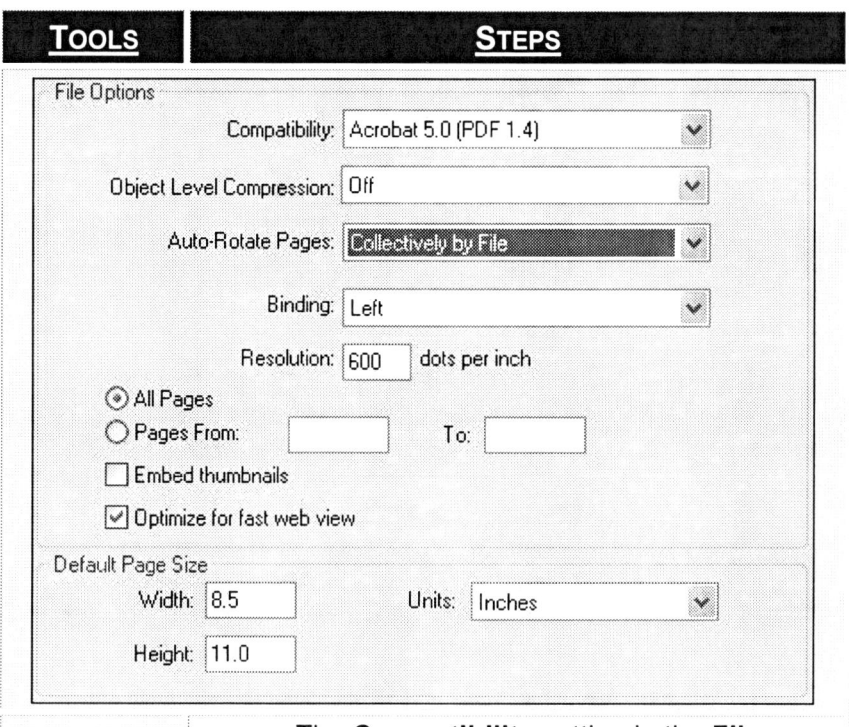

TOOLS	STEPS
File Options 　　Compatibility: Acrobat 5.0 (PDF 1.4) 　　Object Level Compression: Off 　　Auto-Rotate Pages: Collectively by File 　　Binding: Left 　　Resolution: 600 dots per inch 　　⦿ All Pages 　　○ Pages From: ☐ To: ☐ 　　☐ Embed thumbnails 　　☑ Optimize for fast web view Default Page Size 　　Width: 8.5　　Units: Inches 　　Height: 11.0	• The **Compatibility** setting in the **File Options** frame defaults to Acrobat 5.0 (PDF 1.4). As the **Description** explains, this is optimal for viewing with Acrobat 5.0. As the current free Adobe Reader has no problems with this format, we'll accept this setting. • Turn the **Object Level Compression Off** so that your readers can use links and bookmarks. Compressing some objects may save a bit on file size ... but not much. Compressing **Tags only** (the other option) makes links and bookmarks available to Adobe Reader 6.0 users, but not to 5.0. • We won't be rotating pages for our eBook, so the **Auto-Rotate Pages** setting doesn't

Tools	Steps
	mean anything to us. If you're creating an eBook with a lot of tables that required reading from the side (sometimes easier with a handheld device) you can select the **Individually** option.
• **Binding** won't matter in an eBook, but accept the default (**Left**) if you intend to create a POD.
• Accept the default **600** dpi (dots per inch) resolution. You can use a higher resolution (contemporary monitors can generally handle twice that), but unless you're publishing an art book, this resolution handles graphics and text quite nicely. It prints well, too, but your POD house will probably have you set things up to use an even lower resolution.
• Accept the default pages (**All Pages**) unless you just want to create a partial eBook. (Sometimes, I find myself having to reprint just a page or two for reinsertion. This option helps on those occasions.)
• I'd leave the **Embed Thumbnails** box unchecked. Adobe Reader and Acrobat 5.0 and 6.0 dynamically generate a thumbnail for each page (for viewing in the **Pages** pane), so they won't need thumbnails embedded. Earlier readers might not, but the upgrades are free.
• I always **Optimize** [my eBooks] **for fast web view** (even though I don't post my eBooks for viewing on the web). It compresses text and reduces file size.
• Again, accept the **Default Page Size** (in

TOOLS	STEPS
	Points or **Inches**). You can crop later if you must (but remember that Lightning Source and the POD houses require that you use the standard 8½" x 11" page size).
	3. I'll make the **Images** folder/tab (following figure) easy for you; accept all the defaults! This sheet controls Adobe Acrobat's automatic adjustments of the resolution of graphics within your eBook. Many graphics come in very large file sizes and cause your eBook to become too large for the average person to manage. The tendency of most new writers is to accept the larger file sizes to gain "absolute clarity" in their graphics. But the average reader won't notice the difference between 150dpi and 600dpi on a computer screen or in print, so don't go overboard. POD houses generally require the default settings anyway.

TOOLS	STEPS

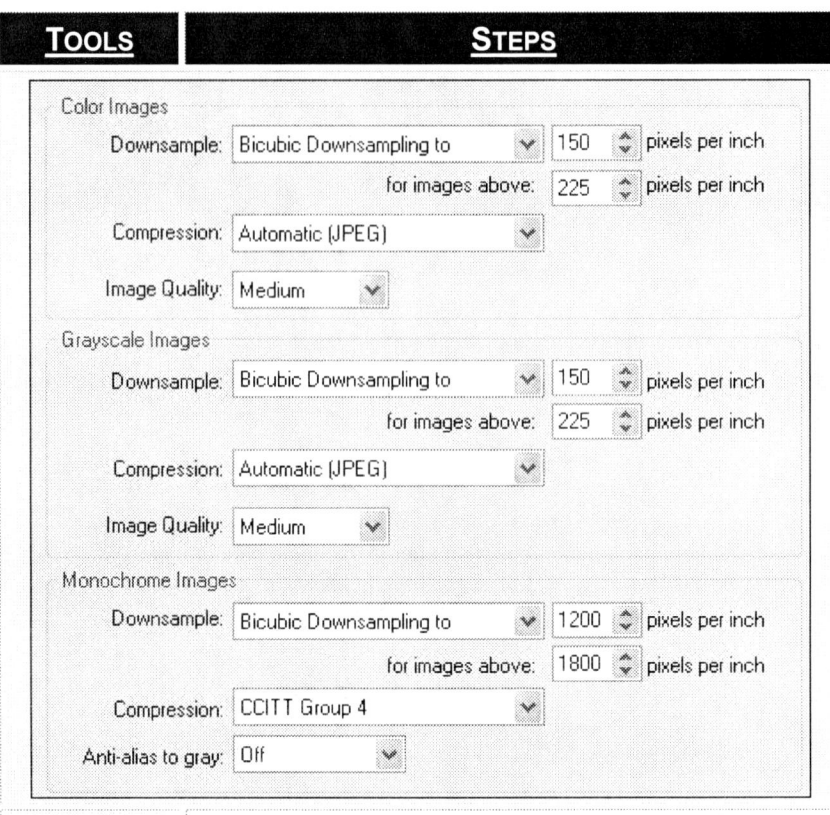

Color Images
Downsample: Bicubic Downsampling to 150 pixels per inch
for images above: 225 pixels per inch
Compression: Automatic (JPEG)
Image Quality: Medium

Grayscale Images
Downsample: Bicubic Downsampling to 150 pixels per inch
for images above: 225 pixels per inch
Compression: Automatic (JPEG)
Image Quality: Medium

Monochrome Images
Downsample: Bicubic Downsampling to 1200 pixels per inch
for images above: 1800 pixels per inch
Compression: CCITT Group 4
Anti-alias to gray: Off

4. Despite its complex appearance, the **Fonts** folder/tab (following figure) has only two important (critical) things of interest to you.

- Lightning Source and the POD houses require that you **Embed all fonts** (luckily, the default setting). If you use any type of non-standard font or text style without embedding it – *you will hear about it and it may increase your setup costs!* Even if you go your own way and don't use LSI or a POD house, your reader will fuss if his copy of your eBook doesn't look exactly like yours.
- **Subset embedded fonts when percent of characters used is less than 100%**

TOOLS	STEPS
	means that Adobe Acrobat will embed only the particular font characters you use. Leave this box checked to help reduce the size of your eBook. (If unchecked or if the percentage entered is reduced below the percentage of the font used in your eBook, Adobe Acrobat will embed the entire font family! Your file size may increase dramatically.)
	With these items checked, you can ignore the rest of the tab.

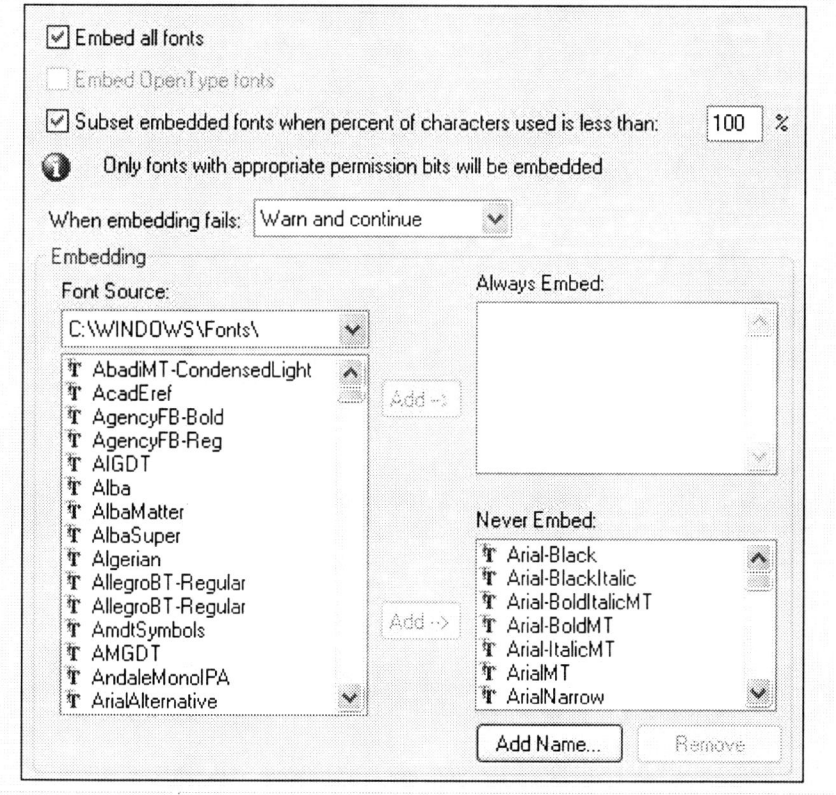

☑ Embed all fonts
☐ Embed OpenType fonts
☑ Subset embedded fonts when percent of characters used is less than: 100 %

Only fonts with appropriate permission bits will be embedded

When embedding fails: Warn and continue

Embedding

Font Source:
C:\WINDOWS\Fonts\

- AbadiMT-CondensedLight
- AcadEref
- AgencyFB-Bold
- AgencyFB-Reg
- AIGDT
- Alba
- AlbaMatter
- AlbaSuper
- Algerian
- AllegroBT-Regular
- AllegroBT-Regular
- AmdtSymbols
- AMGDT
- AndaleMonoIPA
- ArialAlternative

Always Embed:

Never Embed:
- Arial-Black
- Arial-BlackItalic
- Arial-BoldItalicMT
- Arial-BoldMT
- Arial-ItalicMT
- ArialMT
- ArialNarrow

Add Name...   Remove

5. Use the **Color** folder/tab to manage colors. I strongly suggest leaving this tab alone

145

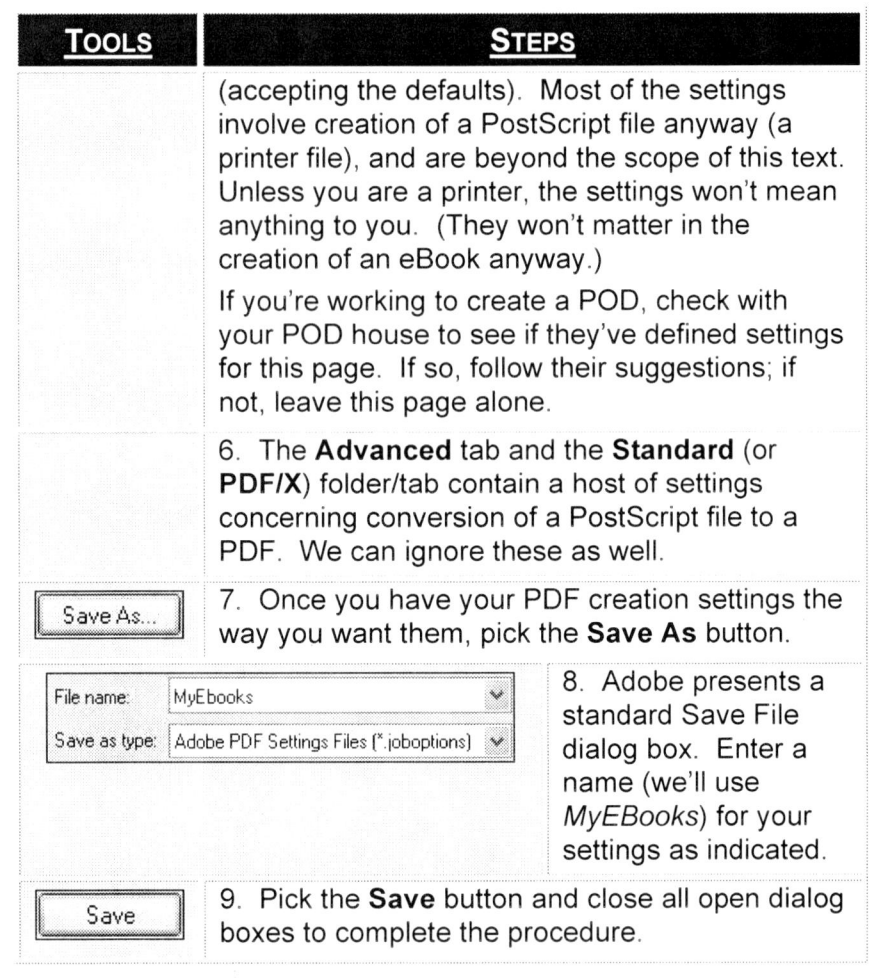

Tools	Steps
	(accepting the defaults). Most of the settings involve creation of a PostScript file anyway (a printer file), and are beyond the scope of this text. Unless you are a printer, the settings won't mean anything to you. (They won't matter in the creation of an eBook anyway.)
	If you're working to create a POD, check with your POD house to see if they've defined settings for this page. If so, follow their suggestions; if not, leave this page alone.
	6. The **Advanced** tab and the **Standard** (or **PDF/X**) folder/tab contain a host of settings concerning conversion of a PostScript file to a PDF. We can ignore these as well.
Save As...	7. Once you have your PDF creation settings the way you want them, pick the **Save As** button.
File name: MyEbooks Save as type: Adobe PDF Settings Files (*.joboptions)	8. Adobe presents a standard Save File dialog box. Enter a name (we'll use *MyEBooks*) for your settings as indicated.
Save	9. Pick the **Save** button and close all open dialog boxes to complete the procedure.

That was probably easier than the length might have led you to believe. But now it's time to do the actual conversion. I'll provide an exercise for each of the setup methods we discussed.

Let's begin.

Do This: 5.2.2.2-A	Converting Your MS Word Document to a PDF Using Adobe Acrobat Imbedded Tools

    i.   Open *Pirates.doc* in MS Word. (I'll use MS Word 2003, but 2000 or 2002 will do as well.)

    ii.   Follow these steps.

TOOLS	STEPS
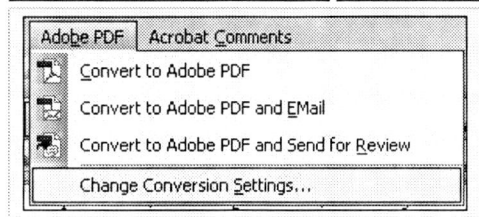 Adobe PDF / Acrobat Comments Convert to Adobe PDF Convert to Adobe PDF and EMail Convert to Adobe PDF and Send for Review Change Conversion Settings...	1. Select **Change Conversion Settings** from the Adobe PDF pull down menu (in MS Word).
	2. MS Word presents the Acrobat PDF Maker with the **Settings** tab on top. (You saw this tab our last exercise.) Select the **MyEBooks** conversion settings you set up in the last exercise (Step 8) as shown in below. (Make sure all the other settings you created in Exercise 5.2.2.1 – Step 1a are still current. If not, please repeat that setup now.)
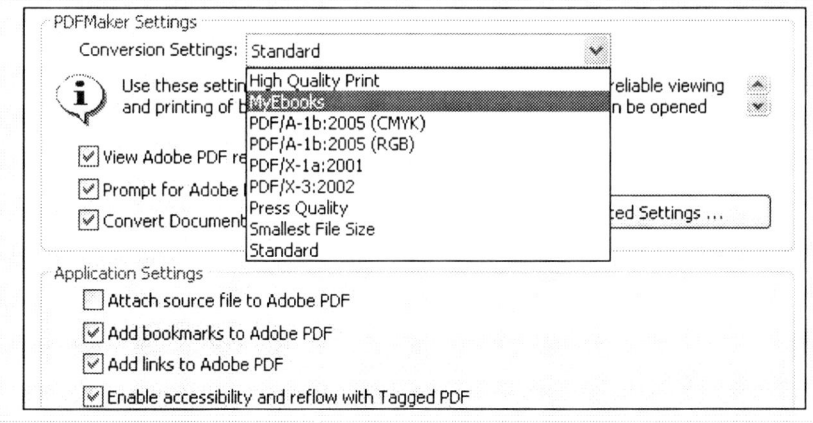 PDFMaker Settings Conversion Settings: Standard High Quality Print **MyEBooks** PDF/A-1b:2005 (CMYK) PDF/A-1b:2005 (RGB) PDF/X-1a:2001 PDF/X-3:2002 Press Quality Smallest File Size Standard ☑ View Adobe PDF re ☑ Prompt for Adobe ☑ Convert Document Application Settings ☐ Attach source file to Adobe PDF ☑ Add bookmarks to Adobe PDF ☑ Add links to Adobe PDF ☑ Enable accessibility and reflow with Tagged PDF	
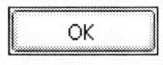 OK	3. Pick the **OK** button to complete this part of the procedure. MS Word closes the PDF Maker.
	4. Pick the **Convert to Adobe PDF** button on the PDFM toolbar. (Adobe placed this toolbar in MS Word when you installed Adobe Acrobat.)

TOOLS	STEPS
	5. Adobe Acrobat prompts for a file name; call it *Pirates-a.pdf*, accept the default location, and proceed with the conversion! (Note: I work with fairly fast computers and, even with this small file, this step takes a few moments.)

Once MS Word and Adobe Acrobat have created your file, it will open in Adobe Acrobat ready for you to begin editing!

Okay, that procedure went smoothly enough. Let's look at creating your PDF using the print command from another application (I'll use WordPerfect 10.0).

Do This: 5.2.2.2-B	Converting Your Document to a PDF Using the Print Command

    i.   Open *Pirates.wpd* in WordPerfect. (Download it from http://foragerpub.com/eBookFiles if necessary.) I'll use WordPerfect 10.0; but this procedure should work as well for other applications. (If you don't have WordPerfect, you can open any document in any other application to complete this exercise. I suggest any non-MS Word document so that you can see the comparison, but a MS Word document will work if that's all you have.)

    ii.   Follow these steps.

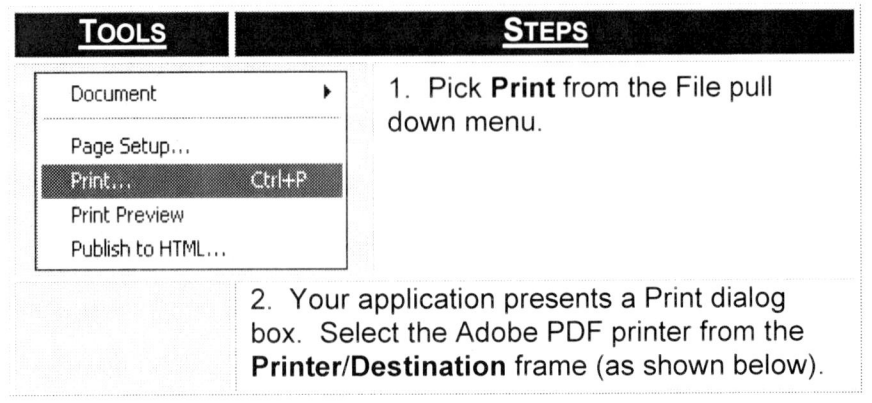

TOOLS	STEPS
Document ▶ Page Setup... **Print...** Ctrl+P Print Preview Publish to HTML...	1. Pick **Print** from the File pull down menu.
	2. Your application presents a Print dialog box. Select the Adobe PDF printer from the **Printer/Destination** frame (as shown below).

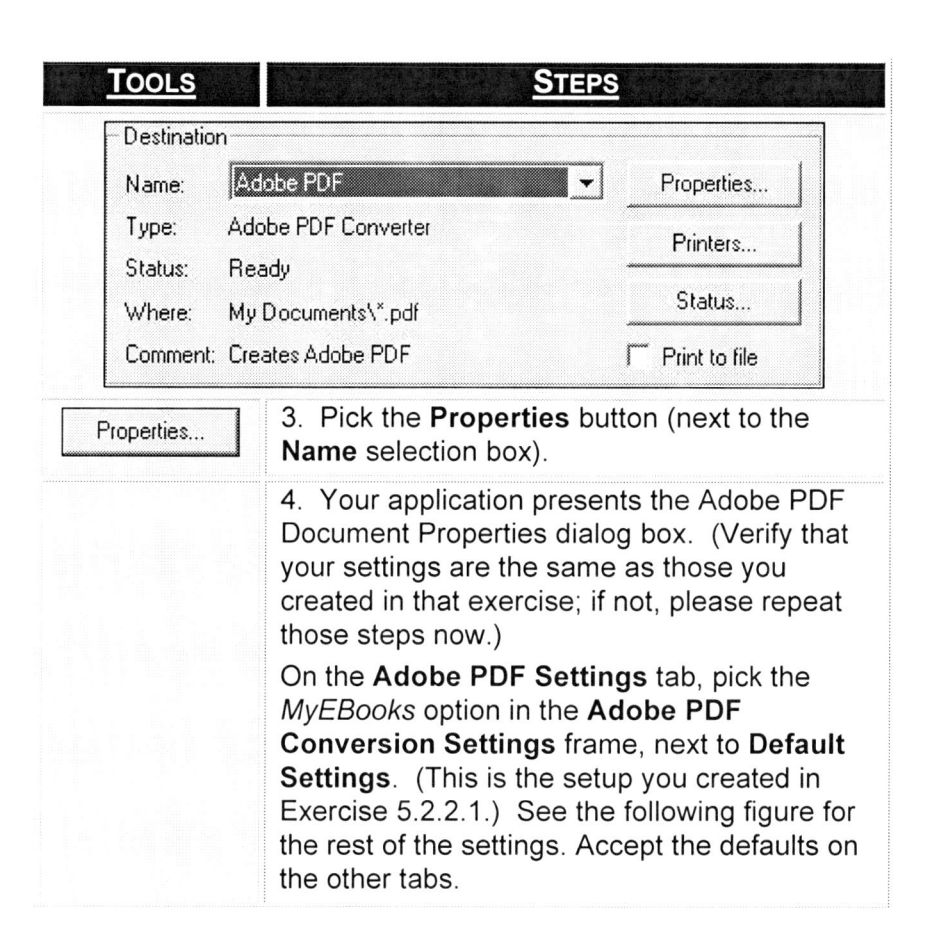

TOOLS	STEPS
![Destination dialog: Name: Adobe PDF; Type: Adobe PDF Converter; Status: Ready; Where: My Documents*.pdf; Comment: Creates Adobe PDF. Buttons: Properties..., Printers..., Status..., Print to file checkbox.]	
Properties...	3. Pick the **Properties** button (next to the **Name** selection box).
	4. Your application presents the Adobe PDF Document Properties dialog box. (Verify that your settings are the same as those you created in that exercise; if not, please repeat those steps now.) On the **Adobe PDF Settings** tab, pick the *MyEBooks* option in the **Adobe PDF Conversion Settings** frame, next to **Default Settings**. (This is the setup you created in Exercise 5.2.2.1.) See the following figure for the rest of the settings. Accept the defaults on the other tabs.

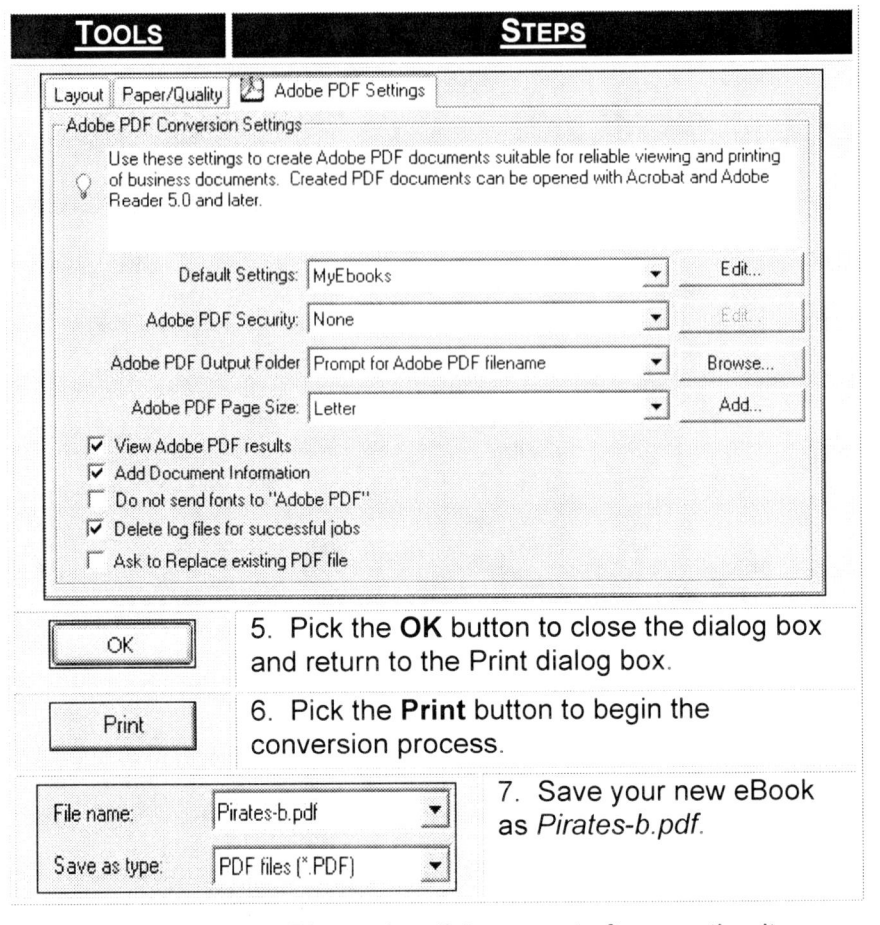

Tools	Steps
[Adobe PDF Settings dialog box showing Layout, Paper/Quality, Adobe PDF Settings tabs. Adobe PDF Conversion Settings: "Use these settings to create Adobe PDF documents suitable for reliable viewing and printing of business documents. Created PDF documents can be opened with Acrobat and Adobe Reader 5.0 and later." Default Settings: MyEbooks. Adobe PDF Security: None. Adobe PDF Output Folder: Prompt for Adobe PDF filename. Adobe PDF Page Size: Letter. Checkboxes: View Adobe PDF results ✓, Add Document Information ✓, Do not send fonts to "Adobe PDF", Delete log files for successful jobs ✓, Ask to Replace existing PDF file.]	
[OK button]	5. Pick the **OK** button to close the dialog box and return to the Print dialog box.
[Print button]	6. Pick the **Print** button to begin the conversion process.
File name: Pirates-b.pdf Save as type: PDF files (*.PDF)	7. Save your new eBook as *Pirates-b.pdf*.

Adobe presents the *Pirates-b.pdf* document after creating it – ready for your review!

You've seen two fairly easy approaches to creating PDFs directly from your word processor (using MS Word embedded commands and using the **Print** command from any other application). Let's take a look at the direct approach.

Do This: **5.2.2.2-C**	**Converting Your Document to a PDF Directly from Adobe Acrobat**

    i.   Open Adobe Acrobat.
    ii. Follow these steps.

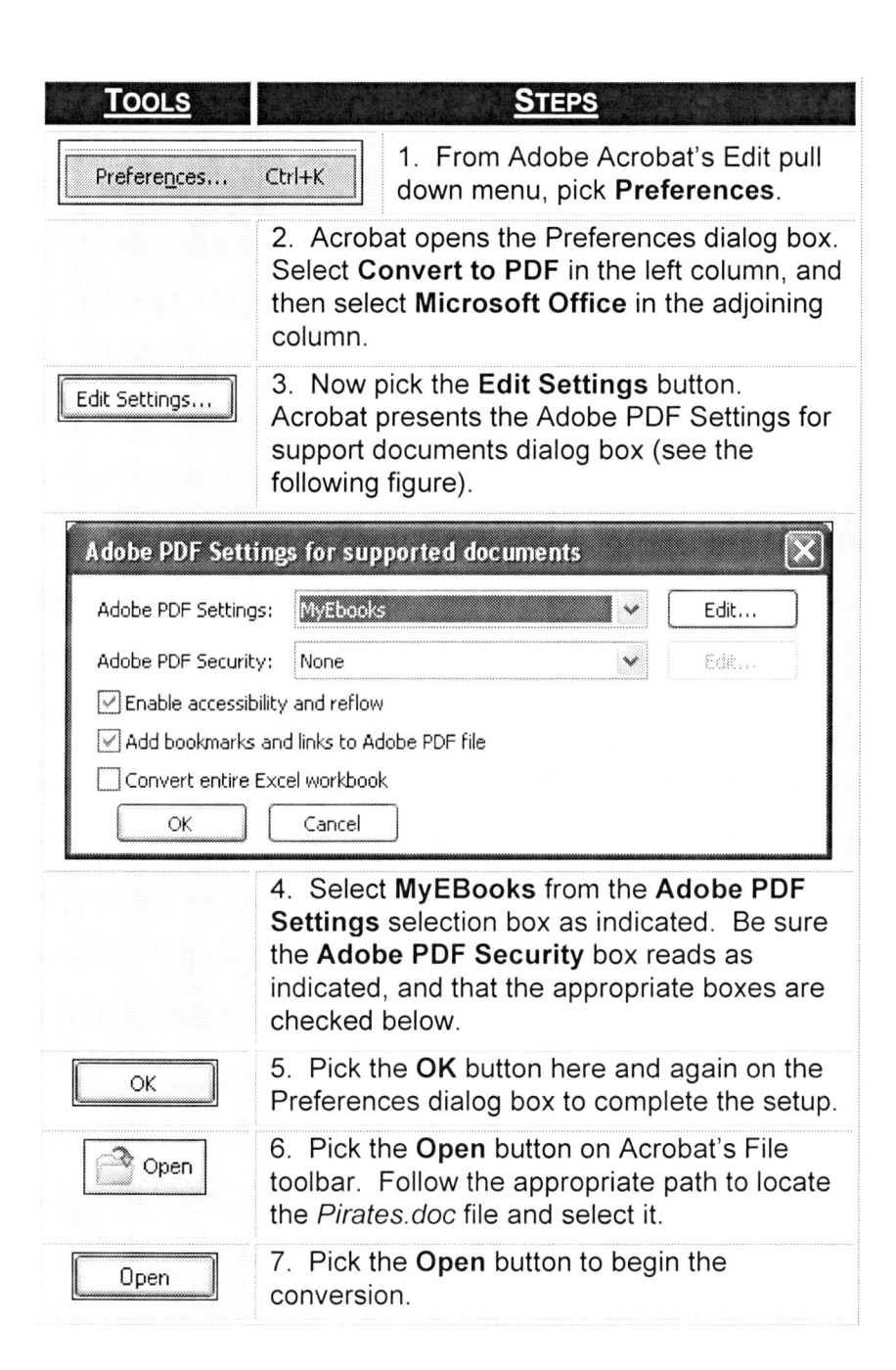

Tools	Steps
Preferences... Ctrl+K	1. From Adobe Acrobat's Edit pull down menu, pick **Preferences**.
	2. Acrobat opens the Preferences dialog box. Select **Convert to PDF** in the left column, and then select **Microsoft Office** in the adjoining column.
Edit Settings...	3. Now pick the **Edit Settings** button. Acrobat presents the Adobe PDF Settings for support documents dialog box (see the following figure).
Adobe PDF Settings for supported documents Adobe PDF Settings: MyEbooks Edit... Adobe PDF Security: None Edit... ☑ Enable accessibility and reflow ☑ Add bookmarks and links to Adobe PDF file ☐ Convert entire Excel workbook OK Cancel	
	4. Select **MyEBooks** from the **Adobe PDF Settings** selection box as indicated. Be sure the **Adobe PDF Security** box reads as indicated, and that the appropriate boxes are checked below.
OK	5. Pick the **OK** button here and again on the Preferences dialog box to complete the setup.
Open	6. Pick the **Open** button on Acrobat's File toolbar. Follow the appropriate path to locate the *Pirates.doc* file and select it.
Open	7. Pick the **Open** button to begin the conversion.

You may have to wait a few moments for the conversion to complete.

> If you receive a "suspicious script" warning from your virus software, tell it to allow the script to run. The conversion process involves some programming that tends to frighten virus software.

Well, that's it! You've created a PDF eBook using three different approaches! (What an experienced publisher you've become!)

Step 5.3 A Word about Post-Conversion Editing

To your list of inevitabilities (death, taxes, the first ding on a new car), you must now add post-conversion editing.

Over the course of the last several years, I've written more than a dozen books ... and have yet to see one hit the market without at least one typo (usually in the most obvious place). Remember what I said about striving for perfection? Well, despite your best efforts, every work of literature – like every child – must eventually be freed to face the world. But (aren't you glad I put a "but" there?) ... BUT, one of the best things about a self-published eBook has to be your ability to fix minor boo boos right up to (and often past) publication! (Unfortunately, your ability to edit a POD – without additional charge – ends when you turn it over to the POD house.)

With Microsoft Reader eBooks, post-conversion editing becomes a chore. We have no tools for editing a .lit file. To edit these eBooks then, you must edit the original manuscript and then recreate the .lit file.

An Adobe file, on the other hand, allows for some minor tweaking provided you have the expertise, training, and software to do it. With Adobe Acrobat Standard or Professional, you can edit text for typos, adjust positioning of text and graphics, add or remove whole pages, and even add or remove hyperlinks! (You may now begin to see why I recommended purchasing the software rather than using the online conversion tool.)

Regardless of which format you've used, I strongly recommend at least one final proofing by you. There's something about the final product that helps you find things that you might have missed in the manuscript. Besides, you'll have to verify positioning of graphics, any centered or indented text (such as poetry or song lyrics within the manuscript), tables, and so forth.

I suggest putting the book aside for a week or two before doing this final reading – to give your mind a rest and allow you to approach the task with a fresh eye. Maybe you can use the time to clean your refrigerator, build a carport, go fishing, or study how to edit a document using Adobe Acrobat.

Step 5.4	Summary

Pat yourself on the back! You've created a book! It's okay to take a moment to bask in some well-deserved pride.

This lesson has taken you from preparation to accomplishment. But your job isn't quite over yet. In fact, the scariest part of all lies ahead! Now that you've created this wonder piece of art, what are you going to do with it?

Don't worry, I won't abandon you here. In Lesson 6, I'll give you a bit of a shove toward the marketing world. There, you'll make your eBook and your POD available for the world ... and take your first tenuous steps toward letting the world know it's there!

Expenses Associated with this Lesson		
Item	Expense (USD)	
	Min	Suggested	Max
None			

Lesson 6

Following this lesson, you will:

- ✓ Know what to expect from POD & eBook Publishers and Distributors
  - o Setting up with Lightning source, Amazon.com, Baker & Taylor, or a POD house
  - o Setting a price
  - o Know your representatives ... and your rights!
  - o Getting paid
- ✓ Know something about your other options
  - o CDs
  - o Audio Books

What to Do with Your eBook or POD

In many ways, I believe that writing a book is the easy part of our profession. In fact, if we didn't face the daunting task of marketing, I believe most writers would long ago have told their 15% agents and their 90% publishers to go ... well, you get the general idea.

Perhaps the computer age will help us all along that road to creative (and financial) independence.

Have you ever read *Moby Dick*? Or like most people, did you try and then tire of the wordiness? (A whole chapter to define a whale?! Aw, com'n, Herman!)

In Melville's day, writers were paid by the word. (No, they really didn't talk that much in the *olde* days.) Imagine what a modern day proofreader/copyeditor would do with Moby Dick! I wonder how we got from there to my last publisher telling me that my AutoCAD textbook was too long.

Well, it's time to talk about marketing your eBook/POD. After all, an unread book benefits no one.

We'll discuss two approaches to marketing and distribution:

- **Hire it done** – That is, use a POD house, Amazon.com, Lightning Source, eBooks.com, and so forth. But be ready for a major (and often expensive) bubble-burster!
- **Do it yourself** – Put your book on your own website and advertise, advertise, advertise (and hope and pray for success).

(The smart way, of course, is to use both approaches!)

Step 6.1	Marketing and Distribution: What to Expect from the Pros

The list of folks willing to "help" you market your work goes on for miles. Like those agents and publishers who take their pound of flesh, however, most of these folks will leave you without enough to survive in the written world. Remember, no one works for free – and *no one works for you except you!* Remember also that you control the checkbook.

Step 6.1.1	Outlets

Now that I've frightened you, let's compare publishers and distributors. We'll start with the very expensive, who will provide everything you'll need (except readers), and move toward the very inexpensive, who require much more from you.

- **POD Houses** – These include AuthorHouse[107], XLibris[108], iUniverse[109], Publish America[110], and a host of others. We discussed the pluses and minuses of these groups in Lesson 3 (Step 3.3), but it might be a good time to review that section.

  When considering a POD house, bear in mind that, although they offer quite a bit, you don't need (and probably can't afford) it all. Let's take a look at what they offer.

  - **Proofreading & Copyediting** – These are generally extras (when offered at all). Although professionally done, the POD houses charge an arm and a leg for these services. You can probably find someone to do it for less on the web or at a local community college or university.
  - **Listing with Ingram Wholesale Distributors** (POD books only) – This sounds great, but consider the following figure.

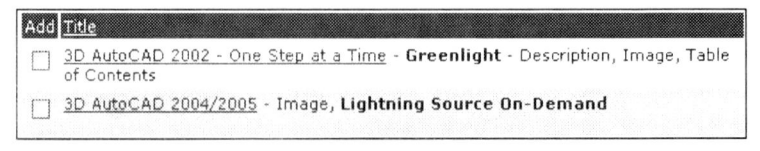

Ingram Listing

This figure displays part of a typical Ingram page. The first listing shows a book published by Prentice Hall;

the second shows a POD book identified as **On-Demand**. Remember how bookstores react to POD books? Well, they fall just below self-published books (vanity press books – which are at least returnable).

Retailers can order your book from Ingram using a page similar to this one, but they will do it only after someone has ordered it from them. Additionally, Lightning Source (as you can see) will list your books with Ingram without the additional expenses of a POD house.

- **Layout** – POD houses shine in this area. They'll do the complete layout – with as much input as you can muster – and save you the hassles of determining proper margins and gutters, forcing graphics where they need to go, creating the PDF for printing or eBook creation, and so forth.
- **Cover** – If you have no artistic ability at all, let your POD house create your cover. They'll generally do a good job and even work with any graphics you'd like to provide. Understand, however, that if you don't like the cover they create, you may have to pay an additional fee to edit or recreate it.
- **Marketing** – Watch out for promises about marketing your book! POD houses offer many options and tools to "assist" you – from the expensive and worthless to the incredibly expensive and almost worthless.

> By the time to get to this point with a POD house, you've already spent hundreds of dollars. You probably haven't seen much (if anything) in returns yet, and you're wondering what you'll have to do to sell your book. Before investing hundreds (or thousands) more, consider the bottom line – how many books will you have to sell to break even with what it's costing you to sell them? Unless you're a marketing professional or an instructor who can require students to buy your book, don't begin by assuming you can sell

thousands (or even hundreds) of books.

Always look for the inexpensive (free!) and unusual way to advertise. And don't be afraid to roll up your sleeves and go sit at a table at the local mall, library, elementary school, etc., reading your POD book, signing autographs, and smiling at the public. Keep a (small) stack of printed books or CDs containing your eBook on hand for impulse buyers!

Let's consider some of the POD houses' marketing offerings.

When dealing with a POD house, be prepared for them to occasionally harass you unmercifully with "opportunities" to spend your money at their establishment.

- A Basic Package includes press release, bookmarks, business cards, and postcards. I chose this package when I published *F'Lump's Adventures with Timmy and Tarbaby* with 1stBooks (now Authorhouse). I received a box of nice printed material, but ...

  There's nothing in this package that you can't do yourself. You have a computer (okay, I assume that most writers in the third millennium have a computer) and a printer. Create your own!

  - Print bookmarks on standard weight paper – 2 3/8"W x 8"L (4/sheet) – and laminate them (use that peel-n-stick laminate if you don't have a laminator). Include a small image of your cover and a brief (150 words +/-) description on the front. Include ordering information on the back.
  - Pick up some precut business cards at your local office supply store. Print a small image of

the cover on the front and 75 words on the back (including ordering information or a web address).
- Do the same with precut postcards (use about 150 words and include ordering information).
- This package may include mailers (press releases) to hundreds of outlets. Most of these will recognize the publisher's name as a POD house and, like the bookstores, will simply ignore it. (If you'd like to write your own press release, you'll find a sample at: http://foragerpub.com/eBookFiles/PressRelease.pdf.)

Bear in mind that, once you've purchased (or created) these items, you'll have to create your own mailing lists and send them out (unless you opt for a more expensive package).

- POD houses offer advertising in *the New York Times Book Review* or some magazine "read by retailers and librarians everywhere." This will gain exposure for your name and the name of your book – alongside thousands of others over the course of a few months. It'll cost you hundreds or even thousands of dollars. (If you have that kind of money, hire a billboard on some major highway – you'll reach as many people and they won't be able to simply scan past your ad!)
- As far as eBooks are concerned, POD houses may offer to list your eBook on their site. But let's face it, how many people other than authors have heard of Authorhouse or Xlibris or iUniverse? You're not going to sell many books there.

Some (Authorhouse.com, contentreserve.com, and bookpublisher.com) will list your eBook at eBooks.com. This web retailer, although new, appears to be growing in popularity. But watch for hidden (and blatant) fees that may be more than you're willing to pay. For example, Authorhouse has fairly recently added a $100 price tag for "electronic distribution" of your book (in addition to the nearly $700 fee for their standard publishing package).

POD houses may also charge a yearly listing fee. (LSI charges $12/year for PODs but nothing for eBooks.) Don't let your POD house charge you too much for this service!

- **Lightning Source** – LSI works for a fraction of the price you can expect to pay a POD house, but they offer almost none of the services. Let's compare.
    - **Proofing and Copyediting, Layout, and Cover** – Not from LSI. By the time your manuscript reaches them, it should be ready for eBook distribution (PDF or Microsoft Reader format) or POD printing. Don't expect them to watch for typos or style/layout errors (they won't even look inside the book).

        That being said, don't confuse not offering services with a lack of quality control for what they do offer. I've had them call about problems with the quality of materials I supplied. I deeply appreciated the catch and opportunity to fix the problem before it went through the cycle.

        > LSI prefers submissions in the Adobe PDF format, but will also accept Adobe PostScript, Quark, and Pagemaker files. For more on their digital requirements, visit their website: https://www.lightningsource.com/ops/files/DigitalFileSubmissions.pdf.
        >
        > For a POD, you can also submit a hard copy for scanning. But ask about additional charges for this service before using it.

    - **Listing with Ingram Wholesale Distributors** (POD books only) – LSI does provide this. In fact, most of the POD houses work through LSI; this is where the listing takes place even if you go through one of them.

- o **Marketing** – LSI offers no help here; but on the other hand, they make no promises either!

> There are a couple points on the downside of LSI: first, they're the only ones doing what they do (providing POD and eBook services to POD houses, and providing eBooks to Amazon.com). You don't have a lot of choice if you're not pleased with their work. Second, they demand immediate payment for their services while waiting four months to provide payment to you for your product. (In their defense, the immediate-demand/four-month-payout trick seems to be common in the distributor world.)

- **Baker & Taylor** – Like Ingram, BTOL distributes printed books to various bookstores and other outlets. (They won't be much help for your eBooks.) Their two divisions work with libraries (including schools and public libraries), and retailers (including traditional, internet, domestic and international retailers). But you'll have to contact BTOL yourself; they don't work directly with most POD houses or LSI. Start at their website: http://www.btol.com.

  Baker and Taylor purchases your books directly from you (you must allow for returns on their purchases to do business with them) and sells to their outlets. They will take the usual 55% commission on your retail price, but they'll pay for what they purchase (they are *not* consignment sellers). Unfortunately, like other purchasers, you'll have to wait for four months to receive your payment. This can be a long four months if they've purchased hundreds (or thousands) or dollars worth of books! (Remember, your printer or POD house wants their money immediately!)

> I really hate to be hypercritical, but I've had problems with BTOL when it comes to getting paid for my books. My personal decision has been to simply not deal with them anymore. Maybe your experience will be better.

- **Amazon.com (and other Internet retailers)** – Amazon.com provides the best outlet for your eBook or POD efforts. It's extremely popular, pays at the end of the month following the sale (they can pay you through their Advantage program[111], or your distributor ... who might take four months to pass it on to you), and they'll work directly with you as a publisher. Other sites, such as eBooks.com, Barnes and Nobles (bn.com), and Powells.com won't.

    To sell your eBook via Amazon.com, you must go through LSI; Amazon simply won't consider any other approach. But this works in your favor. LSI supplies the security and availability for downloads at a reasonable price, and (most importantly) you still get your 45% (LSI and Amazon divvy up the rest for their efforts – including any discounts Amazon offers).

    On the other hand, you can sell your book as an eBook on a CD, audio CD, or self-printed book directly through Amazon's Advantage program. I strongly recommend joining the Advantage program regardless of how you sell your book.

    > As an author or publisher, you gain access to your book's listing at Amazon.com via their Advantage program. Through this program, you can add/change cover graphics, publisher descriptions, author descriptions, and other details about your book to your book's listing. Plus you have the added *advantage* of being able to work directly with those who are selling your book!
    >
    > Before joining the Advantage program, however, be aware that Amazon.com works with you as a consignment seller. That is, you send them your product (book) and they pay you when it sells ... not before! You'll have some inventory tied up this way, but usually not more than a few books unless they're selling "like hotcakes!" If that's the case, smile with each request for more books!

> The Advantage program comes at a flat rate of $29.95/year to list all of your books, plus the usual 55% commission. But this may be the best thirty bucks you invest in your book!

Content Reserve[112] works with eBooks.com in much the same way LSI works with Amazon.com. Unfortunately, the relationship between Content Reserve and eBooks.com appears a bit strained (the eBooks.com representative to whom I communicated no longer recommends Content Reserve since CR has begun charging their authors/publisher a fee to list their material).

> To help you compare:
>
> Content Reserve's commission rate is 50% to 55% with a variable quarterly rate for listing your books. This rate varies according to the number of books you have listed with them. Here's the price list they provided (remember, this is a *quarterly* rate[*]):
>
> > 1 to 10 $75
> > 11 to 25 $125
> > 26 to 50 $250
> > 51 to 100 $375
> > 101 to 250 $625
> > 251 to 500 $1,125
> > 501 to 1,000 $1,875
> > 1,001 to 2,500 $3,375
> > 2,501 to 5,000 $6,250
>
> CR also reserves veto rights over what you can list with them. That is, before accepting your work, they will "determine that the products that you offer meet the needs of our global retail and library buyers." ("Quelle hoity toity," you say? Precisely!)
>
> Although their quarterly price includes a web site, it doesn't include the additional 50% to 55% commission

---

[*] I tried to get more current pricing from Content Reserve for this edition but they didn't answer my email. I'll leave it to you to decide what this says about the company.

> they'll take. I don't recommend using Content Reserve – too many other businesses provide better services for lower prices.

- **Bowker** – When you go through Bowker to get your ISBN, they'll list your title in several databases including BooksInPrint[113] and BookWire[114]. Retail outlets and libraries use these useful tools when looking for title and publisher information. They also offer a host of advertising opportunities,[115] which might facilitate ordering from many retailers.

  I haven't used Bowker for marketing purposes beyond the listings that they include with the purchase of ISBNs. Letting retailers know where they can order my book when they've never heard of my book doesn't seem to be the smart way to invest my marketing capital. Still, purchasing my ISBNs from Bowker makes my information available to retailers once they have heard of my books. So I consider this a better than average source for ISBNs.

- **Local Bookstores (and other outlets)** – Never underestimate the value of your own neighborhood! (No, that doesn't mean going door-to-door ... although I haven't tried that approach yet!)

  Small bookstores can be quite amenable to selling your PODs. Approach them as a local author, offer to do a free reading at their store, agree to sell on consignment, offer to provide a simple display for your books ... but don't pressure them! If they appear uninterested (as many will), simply "shake the dust from your sandals" as you leave. (Promise yourself that, one day, they'll be paying top dollar for your work!)

  Larger bookstores (Barnes & Nobles and their ilk) are less open to local authors – especially POD publishers!

> It's a bookstore, right? They wouldn't mind posting a simple flyer inviting folks to a website for an eBook, right? Think again! Don't expect store owners – of any kind – to encourage folks to shop the Internet.

> The same goes for libraries. That's like asking the dog to encourage the cat to eat bones ... they just don't need the competition.

On the other hand (there's always another hand), keep your eyes open for opportunities! Offer free readings at schools of any and all kinds! (Okay, maybe offering to read your poetry at the local welding academy might not work out, but you get the idea.) Elementary and Middle schools work quite well for children's books (always bring a freebie for the teacher, principal, and librarian). Readings of a more adult nature might fit in at the local community college hangout or writers' guild.

You might also look into local or state-wide book festivals or co-ops.

> The one thing all of these non-Internet related suggestions have in common is this, *you need to have something tangible to sell.* If you've opted to produce strictly an eBook (no POD), then your options are limited.
>
> I once put my 2004 AutoCAD texts on a CD with a nice cover to take with me to readings or sales outings. I sold them at a discounted price via my own website as well. Unfortunately, I suffered terribly from the bootleggers desire to get something for nothing.
>
> I won't do that again!

Don't limit yourself to these marketing tips. Be innovative; be clever! And most importantly, if you come up with a winning approach to sell *your* books, *let me know what it is!*

Step 6.1.2	Pricing

The trick is to under price everyone, right?! I mean, it's an eBook ... it doesn't cost me anything, so it's all profit, right?!

Well, the definitive answer is 'yes' and 'no'. I'm afraid it just isn't that simple.

Let's think about this. If you sold your book to a "real" publisher (Simon and Shuster or Dell Books or McGraw-Hill or some big name company), you'd probably make somewhere between 3% and 12% of their gross. In the case of my AutoCAD books (which retailed for about $45 to $64), this meant about $2 to $3.50 each for me. Of course, Prentice Hall sold a bunch of books.

How should I price my eBook or POD to match (or even better) that?

- **My EBook Price** – eBook pricing is fairly easy. If you want to make $4.50 per book (better than the big houses would pay), divide 4.50 by .45 (or the percentage – in decimal format – that you get to keep after LSI or Amazon or whoever gets their share).

    $$4.5/.45 = 10$$

    The price of your eBook will be $10.00.

    But don't stop there; consider the psychology of the figure $10.00 as opposed to $9.95. With a $9.95 price tag, you can advertise that your eBooks sell for "under $10". The difference to you - $0.02! (You might be surprised how well this works out.)

    Now consider the size of your eBook. My AutoCAD books were too large to convert to a single eBook, so I broke them up into Part I and Part II – each selling for "under $10". This benefited my readers by cutting the price of my books dramatically below what Prentice Hall asked for earlier versions, while making it even easier by splitting the $19.90 final price into two easy purchases (which could be spaced out to further ease the strain on the reader's purse).

    What did the final outcome mean to me? The $3.00 or so I was making for a basic AutoCAD text with a mega-publisher became $8.98! (Okay, before you run out and fire your publisher, remember that I don't sell as many books as did Prentice Hall. Still, I feel that the trade off has been favorable to me.)

- **My POD Price** – You may find POD pricing a bit more difficult to determine. You may also be a bit surprised (and even a bit disappointed) at how close you find yourself to the pricing set by those mega-publishers.

The first number in your equation will be the cost to actually print a book. The POD houses will determine your wholesale pricing based on the number of books you order (generally, go for at least 100, but never for less than 25 if you want to be prudent in your costs). You'll get another number for books sold individually (on-demand) to retail outlets. LSI will do something similar, although the quantity ordered won't affect the pricing until you order more than 500 books.

Always use the greater of these numbers to determine your pricing. I'll use LSI pricing for my 284-page SF novel – *The Vortex*.

Wholesale price (each)	$5.22
handling fee	+ 1.50
Shipping for 25 copies	+ 8.38
Total Wholesale price for 25 books	**$140.38**

This works out to a cost of $5.62 per book. Sound good? But wait ... don't order yet!

Add to this number the amount you'd like to make per book (let's stick with the $4.50 we made on the AutoCAD books).

Cost per book	$5.62
My take	+ 4.50
New cost per book	**$10.12**

Humph. Well, it's still better than what the mega-publishers ask for their books. But wait ... (oh, there's more?).

You can sell your books at the local book fairs, your web site, to local schools, (etc.) for this price and be happy. But what if you want Amazon.com or someone else to sell it for you? You'll have to add their 55%. (Note: The easy way to do the math is to divide your cost per book by your 45% – or .45.)

Cost per book	$10.12
Retailers 55%	+ 12.37
New cost per book	**$22.49**

Aye, carumba!

So, now it's time to be more realistic about the only thing you control out of all these numbers – your take. Let's work backward to see how much I actually get from the sale of *The Vortex*.

Price of the book	$15.85
Retailers 55%	- 8.72
Cost per book	- 5.62
My Take	**$1.51**

Now before you get your knickers in a twist, let's consider this the way a mega-publisher would.

The net for the book (price of the book less the retailers cost) is $7.13. Your $1.51 comes to just over 20% royalties! (A more typical royalty for first fiction might be closer to 5% – or about $0.36 per book.)

Do you begin to see why eBooks and PODs are growing in popularity with authors as well as readers?

| Step 6.1.3 | **Know Your Representatives and Your Rights** |

This section – and any discussion about your rights – will contain a bagful of warnings. Pay attention to them! If you have any further questions, don't hesitate to seek professional legal assistance *before signing anything!*

That said, I should also point out that I've never had a

contractual problem with a POD house, publicist, agent, or distributor (knock on wood). I've been fortunate enough to encounter some fine, (mostly) competent people in this industry.

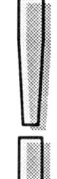

- Never, under any circumstances, assign any rights whatsoever to a POD house. (That's worth repeating – *Never, under any circumstances, assign any rights whatsoever to a POD house.*)
- Furthermore: never, under any circumstances, agree to make a POD house the sole publisher, printer, or distributor of your work.

And finally: never, under any circumstances, agree to allow a POD house to handle anything related to a future work that you may or may not do.

That being said, no reputable POD house will ask for any of these things. Anyone who does, gains quick notoriety throughout the industry and doesn't last for long.

By the time you've written a book, you should (hopefully) have the savvy to know better than to sign anything without reading it first. If not, take that instruction now – *never sign anything without reading it first.* Read your contract carefully – even if you've been graced with a contract from one of those mega-publishers. (I found a couple uh-ohs in my Prentice Hall contract – after the fact – which I might have renegotiated had I stayed with them.)

Leave the shy, reclusive writer in you at home when discussing contracts – ask questions! Make notes on the answers – including who provided them, when, and where. Keep printed copies of emails and letters.

Just as a personal quirk, I always copyright my work personally and before beginning any publishing work. Again, I've never had a problem with losing my work, but this $30 tax-deductible expense goes a long way toward preventing sleepless nights.

Whatever publishing assistance you use, get to know your representative or agent. They're there to help you and are generally accustomed to handling the "tender feelings" of authors.

Most of these folks provide useful insights when asked. I've only found one with whom I had some communication problems, but the company in question quickly replaced this individual with someone else when I requested it. (It doesn't always reflect poorly on the agent and/or author involved; sometimes personalities just don't mesh.)

This brings up another point; remember that you're in charge! It's up to you to follow what's happening with your sales, orders, tracking information, and so forth. Don't expect your agent to volunteer that a shipment has gone awry. (They probably won't know anyway ... until you tell them.) If something goes wrong with an order, let them know as quickly (and as professionally) as possible. Work with them for a solution (one that absolutely does *not* involve your buyer)!

Step 6.1.4	The Payoff – Getting Paid!

We might call an important corollary to this section – *The Payout – Paying Your Bills!*

Always remember that you are a professional – a professional writer (but only you and your readers care about that) *and a professional publisher.* The most unprofessional thing a publisher (or any other professional) can do is to fail to pay his or her bills on time. You can't pout about not being paid for four months and refuse to pay your POD house (or LSI or Amazon.com or other creditor) for an equal amount of time.

When someone orders a book directly from you, expect payment. (You can't go into a bookstore and promise to "pay you on Tuesday for a [textbook] today." Don't let someone do that to you either.) Use the necessary amount of that payment to pay for the books they've ordered.

In many cases, you can save some money in shipping costs by having your POD house or LSI ship directly to your customer.

The rest is your profit.

Many businesses associated with the Internet will ask for your bank account information to directly deposit your earnings. This saves them money in transaction fees, it saves paper (something of no small import to many eBook publishers), and it helps you get paid faster. I haven't run into any problems with Amazon.com or LSI paying me this way. AuthorHouse and Prentice Hall pay by check.

Use your best judgment in deciding how you wish to be paid (if you're given a choice). I'm shy about giving out my personal banking information to anyone, so I set up a business account strictly for Forager Publications. The service charges are deductible.

> Talk to a local CPA before deducting anything, but then deduct everything he says you can! My first year as a freelance writer, I believe I "earned" more in tax deductions than I did in actual income.

Amazon.com will pay by check at your request, but you must first reach a certain amount of earnings (presently $100) before being paid, and they charge $8.00 for the check.

I've mentioned before that many companies pay only after 4 months (LSI, Baker and Taylor); others pay only quarterly (AuthorHouse) or bi-yearly (Prentice Hall). It isn't unusual for some to pay only after a minimum amount of earnings have been met (LSI waits until you've reached $25 in earnings).

Be patient. Don't expect to see three, four, or five figures all at once. (A member of my local writers' guild once told me she went out to eat on her first royalties check – almost paying the entire check at McDonald's! And she went through one of those mega-publishers.)

Those frayed cuffs worn by writers are not the myth you may have thought them to be!

Step 6.1.5	Advertising

Your POD houses will offer to help you advertise in the New York Times (for a few thousand dollars), or they'll write a press release and send it to as many (well, a hundred or so anyway) well-know newspapers or magazines as you can name. But a press release isn't advertising; it's an announcement to people who receive (and often ignore) dozens of press releases a week.

The bottom line to advertising – unless you have one of those mega-publishers on your side (*and often, even when you do*) – is that no one can or will do it for you. (I know, but how many Stephen Kings are there ... and finding someone to spend millions of dollars to advertise your version of *Harry Potter* likely won't happen.)

Unfortunately, advertising doesn't come free; but you can lower the cost. Here's what I've learned so far (although I admit to having far still to go, most of these suggestions will work for eBooks and PODs):

- Never, under any circumstances, spam. Put more simply, don't use email to advertise at all. People don't read spam, and they often block the sender so you won't be able to communicate with the recipient later. Spam houses (millions of mailings for $30!) just make people mad ... even when they're legitimate.

- Web sites work well, although it takes a long time for your listing to appear even after you register with the various search engines. Speak with your web site host about how to register, but don't go with the *$30-to-register-with-a-bazillion-engines* approach. That doesn't help. Take the free registration approach.

  > If you select XO[116] as your host, you can use their **Submit My Site** page to register with several search engines. Alternately, you can use these links: *Google*[117], *AltaVista*[118], *AOL Netfind*[119], *Ask Jeeves*[120], *Looksmart*[121], *Netscape*[122], *Yahoo*[123], and *Overture*[124].

  It will take some time to fill out all the forms (unfortunately, web engines don't share information), but take the time to do it. Eventually (maybe months or even a year or two), it'll pay off.

- Create targeted mailing lists – schools, homeschool organizations, writers clubs, Science Fiction clubs, arboreta, and so forth. Perhaps your best target might be specific departments of colleges and universities, high schools, or even elementary schools. There you'll find concentrations of people interested in specific topics. (I'd ignore bookstores – except those affiliated with a specific site like an arboretum or a science museum. I'd also ignore libraries – they find their books in catalogs.)

Find your targets with web searches (or search through phone books), and write down mailing addresses (with zip codes). Start a data base (or make a nice list) of the names and addresses. MS Word has a nice mail-merge tool that will take the addresses from your data base and print out sheets of address labels.

Once you have a mailing list, send a nice post card. You can easily and inexpensively print these on your home computer. Take some time in the design of these cards; put a picture of your cover on the front, and a nice teaser with an invitation to your web site – or even your site at Amazon.com – for more details on the back.

- I've never advertised in a big magazine and made enough money from the effort to pay for the ad. You may have better luck, but I can't recommend spending tight advertising dollars on small ads in big magazines.
- I have had some success in buying medium sized ads in well-targeted newsletters. These generally hit a small but relatively avid audience in a specific area (my children's audio books did well with ads in a few homeschool newsletters).
- Don't be shy about dropping a free children's book (or CD for an eBook) at the local elementary school library. Take a few minutes while you're there to visit with the librarian and offer to do a reading from your book. Don't charge the first few times you do this – build your reputation. (Don't charge more than gas money even when you're well-

known in the area. You can make money by passing out flyers to the students/teachers/parents with details for buying your book.) And don't press the librarian on the reading; she doesn't know you from Adam (or Eve) and will have to look at your book and ask around about you.

- Do public readings whenever and wherever you can. Many bookstores won't be interested in a POD reading, but some smaller ones will. Elementary schools and daycares are good locations, too (bring some little freebies for the kids – stickers with pictures of your characters are good; candy is not).
- Take your printed books (or eBook CDs) to local book fairs. Sometimes you'll make some money; sometimes you won't. But you'll meet other writers doing the same thing you're doing and have a chance to discuss new ideas with them. Besides, book fairs are fun! The host will often list your name and title(s) in their advertising, too!
- I once contacted an advertising firm to help me market my children's books. The reception I got was lukewarm at best. Okay, I only had so much to invest and it wouldn't pay for the agent's well-coiffed hair (much less her new car), so I suppose I should have expected what I got in ideas/proposals (nothing). Still, it's another possibility you can try if you're well-healed and willing to spend the dough.

I'm sure you can find plenty of ways to advertise your book that I haven't mentioned here. (Let me know if you find a guaranteed winner!)

I strongly suggest determining how much you have to spend on advertising before you even begin considering the possibilities. Create a budget for it – so much per month. Then (very importantly) *stick to your budget!* The world teems with temptations and those willing (and eager) to separate you from your hard-earned money. Consider what I've written here, speak to other writers about things they've done, and then devise a plan!

Step 6.2 Other Options – CDs and Audio Books

Although putting your eBooks on CD takes little effort, I recommend caution in the sale of these CDs. You really want to encourage downloads (via Lightning Source or one of the POD houses) whenever possible for the security they can provide. You can sell your CDs at local book fairs or through your website, but you can't control the number of copies people will make. Still, when you're just beginning, even illegal copies get your name out there! That'll help in the long run when you sell the sequel!

What else is there?

Let's look at audio books – with just a touch of CD creation thrown in for good measure.

What is an audio book?

An audio book is a recorded reading of your book.

Who does the reading?

Well, you could hire Patrick Stewart (Jean-Luc Picard of TV's *Star Trek*) or Orson Wells (oh wait, he's not available anymore), but you're on a budget. Why not read it yourself? (Who can read your book as well as you?)

I know, you're not an actor (actress). But try it. Read a few paragraphs into a tape recorder. Listen to the recording. Repeat the exercise until you're happy with what you hear. Can't get rid of that horrible New England twang? Place an ad on the bulletin board at your local college/community college/university in the Drama Department. Most students would love the chance to get their name credited as reader on an audio book cover (good for their résumé ... and they could use a few bucks, too).

If you decide to read yourself, read with enthusiasm! Pretend you're telling a story to a child or a group of friends who get bored easily.

Okay, you don't know what I mean. Pick up a couple audio books from the local library. (If you've written a children's book, pick up children's audio books; if you've written the world's best romance, pick up a romance or two.) Listen carefully how the reader animates the text with his or her voice. That's your goal!

What format do I use (cassette, CD)?

Use both. It'll probably be easiest to read it onto a cassette recorder, but it'll be harder to edit later. (Yes, audio books need editing, too.)

I do my reading into my computer; I use Magix Audio Studio[125], which sells for about $40. But any good recording software will work. Make sure you get one capable of creating and editing MP3 files (the new rage in sound recording); they're smaller than WAV files (the old standard) and have a better quality. It may take you some time to get comfortable with the procedures involved in creating and editing audio files, so save this task until after you've already published your book.

Once the audio file(s) is created, use your CD burner to put it (them) onto disks. (From the CD, you can record cassettes if you wish.)

How do I sell my recording?

(This information applies to eBooks on CDs as well.)

First, design a nice CD label – use the cover of your book, a byline, copyright notice, etc. Be sure to label disk 1, 2, and so forth. (Check out covers of the audio books available at your local library. You can buy some if you wish, but audio books can be expensive. Try ordering – or even renting – online at BooksOnTape.com[126]. Their prices are reasonable even if their selection could be broader.)

Then design a nice label for your jewel case (the plastic case that holds the CD). Again, use the cover of your book and a teaser on the back. Be sure to place the ISBN and barcode on the back. (Amazon and other retail outlets won't sell it without the barcode.) Of course, if you plan to sell the audio or CD version strictly on your own website, you won't need the ISBN or barcode. (Note: You *cannot* use the same ISBN you used for the eBook or POD version of the book.)

You can purchase blank labels at any office supply store and print them on any laser jet printer. I don't recommend using an ink jet printer, although you can in a crunch. Ink jet ink tends to run or bleed in humid conditions. You can even use those new CD burners that print directly onto the CD, although they're a bit more expensive than buying a few labels.

Price your audio books to sell. Remember, it takes very little money to produce them (unless you had to pay Patrick Stewart), so you can fairly easily under price the mega-publishers. But don't make them too low, either. If you price them too low, buyers will think they're cheap.

> My F'Lump series costs about $2.92 each to put on audio CD. This price includes the three CDs the book requires, and all the packaging. They cost about $1.00 to ship in the US. I sell them at Amazon.com for about $15. After amazon's 55%, I still make about $2.83 each. Of course, selling directly or through my own website means that I can sell them at a discount (say, $10) and make more!

List your audio book on your own website. The profits from selling directly greatly overshadow those sold by retail outlets, although the volume doesn't compare.

| **Step 6.3** | **Summary** |

> *You're on!*
> [My friend Alex when I showed signs
> of stage fright before a class.]

My dad often scolds me about my inabilities to sell a book. I have talent as a writer ... am even a good publisher; but selling has never been my forté. Still, I have managed to sell thousands of books (traditional, POD, and eBook) through Prentice Hall (my mega-publisher) and Forager Publications (my own publishing house). I must be doing something write (*sic*)!

Writing and selling involve entirely different parts of a personality – the introverted and the extroverted. Unfortunately, the two rarely mesh well. So I'll leave you with the anecdote that led to the quote at the head of this section.

As I stood outside a classroom one day, trying in vain to overcome my usual stage fright at the beginning of a new class, my new friend Alex came along and asked me what was wrong. When I explained, she smiled her winning "teacher" smile and told me the solution was simple. I looked at her quizzically, but she simply opened the door, gave me a slight shove, and said, "You're on!"

At that moment, class began. As I was the teacher, everything hinged on what I did next. I could either turn and run (and lose my job) or say, "Hello." I said hello. Then I began talking about the subject of the class – something I knew more about than my students ... and for which I had some enthusiasm. I let the enthusiasm take over and the rest, as they say, is history.

I spoke to Alex later, chiding her for her swim-or-drown approach to my problem. She smiled again (she had a nice smile) and asked what had happened to my stage fright. I told her I had to leave it at the door.

And that's what I'm telling you. When you find yourself trying to sell your book, leave your fears at the door. You know your book ... and you have enthusiasm for it. And now, you're on!

Following is a list of expenses associated with Lesson 6.

Expenses Associated with this Lesson

Item	Expense (USD)		
	Min	**Suggested**	**Max**
LSI Listing fee	0	12/yr	12/yr
Amazon.com Advantage Program	0	29.95/yr	29.95/yr
Website registry	0	0	30
Audio Studio	0	40	?
Marketing & Advertising	0	?	?

Conclusion

... But I have promises to keep,
And miles to go before I sleep.
And miles to go before I sleep.

From "Stopping by Woods on a Snowy Evening"
by Robert Frost

I'll leave you with a few final thoughts.

Like many of you, I dreamed of becoming a writer since childhood. Over the years, I've written more than my share of really bad prose and poetry ... and some good stuff, as well. All the while, I searched for that Holy Grail of freelance writing – a publisher who'd believe in my work enough to publishing it.

I found a few magazines willing to publish articles I'd written (and pay me for the trouble!); I found a few vanity publishers willing to publish some of my poems. I even found a magazine willing to publish a short story once. Then finally, in 1998, I convinced one of those mega publishers to produce my AutoCAD textbooks. These quickly became very popular – remaining in the top ten of AutoCAD textbooks at Amazon.com for years.

I was on my way, at last; but I wasn't satisfied. I was determined to do more, but my mega-publisher wouldn't look at my fiction ... or any of my work that didn't deal directly with AutoCAD. My success, it seemed, had become linear.

It was then that I determined to publish my own work. I began with my children's series – *F'Lump's Adventures with Timmy and Tarbaby*, which I wrote while reading the drafts to a group of third graders at a local elementary school. F'Lump did okay locally and in audio release – despite the occasional reviewer panning my dog's name as being "not PC".

Never one to dwell on the absurd, I did a sequel to F'Lump, and then produced my first Science Fiction – *The Vortex*. I wasn't getting rich, but this was the most fun I'd ever had writing!

Finally, I determined to publish my own AutoCAD texts. I came to an agreement with my mega-publisher to regain the rights to the titles, and produced the last several releases myself.

Since I began about three or four years ago, I've sold several thousand books and eBooks using the approach detailed in this text.

That's the short version of my success story. I'm still not rich, and you may never see my name listed beside Robert Heinlein or Dr. Seuss or the like (then again, maybe ... just maybe you *will*). But I've never been happier in my work.

I still have goals and "miles to go before I sleep", but I'm living that dream at last. I hope this text will help you do the same.

Good Luck!

Tim

Remember: Success Has Its Pluses!

Appendix: Internet Links

You can find this list as actual links in this file:
http://www.foragerpub.com/eBookFiles/Links.pdf

---

[1] http://www.ask.com/
[2] http://www.microsoft.com/reader/developers/downloads/rmr.asp
[3] http://www.adobe.com/products/acrobatstd/main.html
[4] http://www.adobe.com/products/acrobatpro/main.html
[5] https://createpdf.adobe.com/index.pl/1759620944.19278?BP=IE&v=AHP
[6] https://createpdf.adobe.com/index.pl/1759620944.19278?BP=IE&v=AHP
[7] http://www.adobe.com/products/acrobat/readstep2.html
[8] http://www.microsoft.com/reader/downloads/dictionaries.asp
[9] http://www.adobe.com/products/acrobat/pdfs/acrruserguide.pdf
[10] http://www.adobe.com/products/acrobat/readstep2.html
[11] http://www.microsoft.com/reader/downloads/
[12] http://www.microsoft.com/reader/developers/downloads/tts.asp
[13] http://www.microsoft.com/reader/downloads/dictionaries.asp
[14] http://www.microsoft.com/reader/downloads/dictionaries.asp
[15] http://digitalmediastore.adobe.com/6D2F4505-8CDF-4562-A4F2-B7CE1CFF5D8C/10/21/en/Default.htm
[16] http://digitalmediastore.adobe.com/6D2F4505-8CDF-4562-A4F2-B7CE1CFF5D8C/10/21/en/Default.htm
[17] http://www.amazon.com/exec/obidos/tg/browse/-/551440/ref=b_tn_bh_eb/104-4823952-4931922
[18] http://www.powells.com/ebookstore/ebooks.html
[19] http://www.fictionwise.com/
[20] http://us.ebooks.com/
[21] http://www.ebookdirectory.com/
[22] https://www.lightningsource.com/
[23] http://www.authorhouse.com/home.aspx
[24] http://www2.xlibris.com/
[25] http://www.iuniverse.com/
[26] http://www.microsoft.com/office/word/prodinfo/default.mspx
[27] http://www.adobe.com/products/acrobatstd/main.html
[28] http://www.adobe.com/products/acrobatpro/main.html
[29] http://www.microsoft.com/reader/developers/downloads/rmr.asp
[30] http://www.microsoft.com/traincert/training/find/findcourse.asp
[31] http://www.microsoft.com/office/word/howtobuy/default.mspx
[32] http://office.microsoft.com/home/default.aspx

[33] http://www.corel.com/servlet/Satellite?pagename=Corel2/Products/Home&pid=1047022958453
[34] http://apps.corel.com/partners_directory/Training_Partner_Directory/default.asp
[35] http://www.corel.com/servlet/Satellite?pagename=Corel2/Products/Home&pid=1047022958453
[36] http://www.adobe.com/products/acrobatstd/main.html
[37] http://www.adobe.com/products/acrobatpro/main.html
[38] https://createpdf.adobe.com/index.pl/1759620944.19278?BP=IE&v=AHP
[39] http://www.amazon.com/exec/obidos/tg/detail/-/0321247434/qid=1086880611/sr=1-8/ref=sr_1_8/002-1406390-2985616?v=glance&s=books
[40] http://www.amazon.com/exec/obidos/tg/detail/-/0072229462/qid=1086880659/sr=1-1/ref=sr_1_1/002-1406390-2985616?v=glance&s=books
[41] http://www.microsoft.com/reader/developers/downloads/rmr.asp
[42] http://clipart.com/en/index
[43] http://www.e-frontier.com/article/articleview/1597/1/281?sbss=281
[44] http://www.e-frontier.com/article/articleview/1597/1/281?sbss=281
[45] http://www.amazon.com/gp/product/B000AMFBSY/qid=1146081071/sr=12-1/104-7619895-5150340?s=books&v=glance&n=551440
[46] http://www.daz3d.com/
[47] http://www.renderosity.com
[48] http://www.corel.com/servlet/Satellite?pagename=Corel3/Products/Display&pfid=1047024307383&pid=1047025487586
[49] http://www.adobe.com/products/photoshop/main.html
[50] http://www.corel.com/servlet/Satellite?pagename=Corel3/Trials/Login&pid=1047025487586&cid=1047025490241
[51] https://www.lightningsource.com/
[52] https://www.lightningsource.com/LSISecure/PubResources/SpineCalcCriteria.aspx?App=WWW
[53] https://www.lightningsource.com/LSISecure/PubResources/CoverSpecsEntry.asp
[54] http://www.amazon.com/gp/search/ref=nb_ss_eb/102-9264409-7197741?url=search-alias%3Debooks&field-keywords=&Go.x=9&Go.y=14
[55] http://www.simplyenglish.com/rate.htm
[56] http://www.creative-editor.com/
[57] http://www.acecopyediting.com/
[58] http://www.isbn.org/standards/home/index.asp
[59] https://www.lightningsource.com/

[60] http://www.copyright.gov/forms/formtxs.pdf
[61] http://www.copyright.gov/forms/formtxi.pdf
[62] http://www.copyright.gov/circs/circ03.pdf
[63] http://www.copyright.gov/
[64] http://cip.loc.gov/
[65] http://pcn.loc.gov/
[66] http://www.loc.gov/issn/issnbro.html
[67] http://www.isbn.org/standards/home/isbn/us/san/index.asp
[68] http://www.pageresource.com/html/index.html
[69] http://www.amazon.com/exec/obidos/tg/detail/-/0672325209/qid=1088511866/sr=1-5/ref=sr_1_5/104-4428182-0340734?v=glance&s=books
[70] http://www.xo.com/products/smallgrowing/hosting/websites/
[71] http://www.webhosting.com/
[72] http://www.earthlinkhosting.net/
[73] http://cheapdomain.com/
[74] http://register.com/
[75] http://www.microsoft.com/smallbusiness/online/web-hosting/detail.mspx
[76] http://www.foragerpub.com/
[77] http://www.uneedcad.com/
[78] http://cheapdomain.com/
[79] http://register.com/
[80] http://www.ftpx.com/
[81] http://www.google.com/addurl.html
[82] http://www.altavista.com/addurl/default
[83] http://tools.search.aol.com/tools/index.html
[84] http://ask.ineedhits.com/
[85] http://listings.looksmart.com/home/contact.jhtml
[86] http://wp.netscape.com/escapes/search/addsite.html
[87] http://search.yahoo.com/info/submit.html
[88] https://client.enhance.com/ols/index.do?network=webcrawler
[89] http://www.barnesandnoble.com/
[90] http://www.authorhouse.com/
[91] http://www2.xlibris.com/
[92] http://www.iuniverse.com/
[93] http://www.wheatmark.com/
[94] http://us.ebooks.com/
[95] http://www.amazon.com/
[96] http://www.amazon.com/exec/obidos/subst/partners/direct/direct-application.html/102-5971571-9761730

[97] http://www.amazon.com/gp/seller-account/management/your-account.html//102-5971571-9761730
[98] http://www.m-w.com/mw/table/proofrea.htm
[99] http://www.bartleby.com/61/charts/A4proof.html
[100] http://www.microsoft.com/reader/developers/downloads/layout.asp
[101] http://www.microsoft.com/reader/developers/downloads/layout.asp
[102] http://www.microsoft.com/reader/developers/downloads/source.asp
[103] http://www.microsoft.com/reader/developers/downloads/markup.asp
[104] http://www.microsoft.com/reader/developers/partners/conversionproviders.asp
[105] http://www.microsoft.com/reader/developers/downloads/rmr.asp
[106] https://createpdf.adobe.com/index.pl/379402732.602017?BP=IE&v=AHP
[107] http://www.authorhouse.com/home.aspx
[108] http://www1.xlibris.com/
[109] http://www.iuniverse.com/
[110] http://www.publishamerica.com/
[111] http://www.amazon.com/exec/obidos/subst/partners/direct/direct-application.html/103-8871454-8438214
[112] http://www.contentreserve.com/
[113] http://www.booksinprint.com/
[114] http://www.bookwire.com/bookwire/
[115] http://www.bookadvertising.net/adsales/index.htm
[116] http://register.cnchost.com/reg/
[117] http://www.google.com/addurl.html
[118] http://www.altavista.com/addurl/default
[119] http://search.aol.com/aolcom/add.jsp
[120] http://ask.ineedhits.com/
[121] http://listings.looksmart.com/home/contact.jhtml;jsessionid=SEH0Z5MPOXSM5LAQQB2E2LFMCCAHSTRF?leadContactState=2
[122] http://wp.netscape.com/escapes/search/addsite.html?cp=nsistatic
[123] http://help.yahoo.com/help/us/url/
[124] https://signup.overture.com/s/dtc/signup
[125] http://site.magix.net/index.php?id=13469&no_cache=1
[126] http://www.booksontape.com/

Printed in the United States
120034LV00003B/309/A